From the Marshall Plan to COVID-19
James G. Lowenstein at 94

John Seaman

New Publishing Partners
Washington, DC

Copyright © James G. Lowenstein, 2021

Published by New Publishing Partners
2510 Virginia Avenue
Suite 902N
Washington, DC 20037
www.npp-publishing.com

ISBN-13: 978-1-7374940-0-3
ISBN-10: 17374940-0-0

The photos in this book are from the James G. Lowenstein collection

Book design and cover design by Deborah Lange

To my grandchildren—Jake, Haley, and Alex
May my past be their prologue.

Whereof what's past is prologue, what to come
In yours and my discharge.
                              William Shakespeare
                              The Tempest, Act 2, Scene 1

Contents

Acknowledgments 7
Preface 9
Prologue: Early Years 11
1 The Marshall Plan 21
   An American in Paris 21
   An American in Sarajevo 28
   The Three Wise Men 35
2 From the Navy to the Foreign Service 39
   The Navy 39
   A Law School Experiment 46
   A Foreign Service Officer 48
   Office of European Regional Affairs 50
   Ceylon 54
   Back to Yugoslavia 58
3 Capitol Hill 68
   Fulbright and the Senate Foreign Relations Committee ... 68
   "Somebody Wasn't Telling the Truth" 79
   "Not Only Far from Won But Far from Over" 84
   The Power of Information 90
   Other Lowenstein/Moose Investigations 95
   A Never-Ending War 98
   Persistence, Perseverance, and Opportunity 102
4 Return to State 136
   Kissinger's State Department 136
   Forming the French-American Foundation 142
   Luxembourg 146
Epilogue: Later Years 157
   IRC 157
   Writing and Speaking 159
   Election Observer Missions 160
   Serving on Boards 162

The French-American Foundation 163
Octogenarians Without Borders 167
Tennis 168
Travels 168
Family 169
Conclusion 170
Notes 171

Acknowledgments

I want to acknowledge the work done by the author, John Seaman of Saybrook Partners, in putting into historical context the various phases of my life. His diligent research gave the book a dimension that added immeasurably to its narrative.

I also want to express my gratitude to Debbie Lange of New Publishing Partners for her invaluable editing. There are many good editors in the publishing world, but, I suspect, few with her background, experience, sensitivity, and—most importantly—patience. I am much indebted to her.

Finally, I want to thank those who consented to be interviewed for this book. I appreciated their kind words and, even more, their restraint from criticism.

James G. Lowenstein

Preface

This is not a conventional work of biography. It arose out of a wish by its subject, James G. Lowenstein, to record for posterity some of the fascinating observations from his three decades in government service. These reminiscences, he believed, would shed light on the many notable persons, institutions, or events with which he has been involved. He decided that his story was best told from an independent perspective by an author who could put that story in its broader historical context. In 2019, he engaged me as his biographer.

This book is based on professional research, including interviews with Lowenstein and several of his friends and colleagues, an examination of memoranda and other papers in his personal archive, a review of other published accounts (such as memoirs, oral histories, newspapers), and reading in the scholarly and other secondary literature on relevant themes in foreign affairs. The book is not comprehensive. For many of the episodes recounted here, there are no records to consult or people to interview, leaving me to reconstruct the story as best I could from related contemporaneous sources. At Lowenstein's request, I have omitted most of the personal details of his life, such as marriages, children, and friendships, and focused my attention on his professional pursuits.

Lowenstein's long career in foreign affairs makes a compelling story. In its overarching themes and concerns, it reflects in miniature the contours of "the American Century," when United States' global leadership was at its zenith—mostly for good but sometimes for ill. The pages that follow attempt to do justice to Lowenstein's long and eventful life.

John Seaman

Prologue: Early Years

James Gordon Lowenstein was born on August 6, 1927, in Long Branch, New Jersey, and raised in nearby Shrewsbury. He was the eldest son of Melvyn Gordon Lowenstein and his wife, Katherine (née Goldsmith) and had two younger brothers, Hugh and Peter. Shrewsbury was home for the next 10 years, and life there was idyllic for a young boy. During the school year, Lowenstein attended a small private school in neighboring Red Bank. In the summers, family life shifted to Elberon, a village of Long Branch, where his grandparents owned a rambling seaside cottage that had once belonged to President Ulysses S. Grant.

Lowenstein's early years were shaped in important ways by a long and colorful family history with deep roots in America. Lowenstein could trace the American beginnings of his maternal line to October 7, 1755, when Isaac Levy, one of his mother's Jewish forebears, arrived in Philadelphia from Rotterdam on the ship *Neptune* with his wife, Catharine, and their baby girl, Hannah. He took the oath of allegiance the same day. A dry goods merchant, Levy and his business partner, Barnard Jacobs, traded with American colonists and Native Americans alike. A family legend has it that Isaac and Catharine divorced in 1770, at a time when divorce was rare. Other records, however, indicate that Isaac died in 1764, and that Catharine married Barnard Jacobs six years later, after Jacobs' wife had passed away.[1] Hannah Levy married Eleazar Lyons on May 29, 1776. They had seven children and opened a stationery store in Philadelphia, which developed into a book publishing company, Moss and Bro.

A second branch of the maternal line can be traced to 1866, when Louis Goldsmith, also Jewish, arrived in the United States from Oettigen, Bavaria. He had a dry goods business of his own, this one in Portland, Oregon. On occasion, he traveled to New York, which in the years before Portland was connected to the transcontinental railroad, required him to travel nearly 800 miles to Salt Lake City by stagecoach.² Louis had six brothers. One of his older brothers, Bernard, served as Mayor of Portland from 1869 to 1871.

Lowenstein's paternal line in America begins in 1847, when August Lowenstein, also Jewish, emigrated from Bavaria at age 20. A butcher by trade, he settled in Cincinnati, where he went on to own and manage one of the country's early meatpacking plants.

Judaism, however, played little role in Lowenstein's life, for the family's religious identity had begun to lapse well before he was born. Isaac Levy's great-grandson, Joseph Lafayette Moss, was one of some 8,000 American Jews to have fought in the American Civil War, where his bravery earned him speedy promotion to the rank of lieutenant colonel in the 13th Pennsylvania Calvary. Moss was also a proud member of the Freemasons for over 60 years, and when he died in 1906, he was buried on the grounds of the First Presbyterian Church in Metuchen, New Jersey.³

Lowenstein's maternal grandmother, Kate Moss Price Goldsmith, attended services at Temple Emanu-El in New York, but his maternal grandfather, James A. Goldsmith, never set foot there, according to his mother's oral history. Nor did any of the children, including Lowenstein's mother, who raised her family in the same secular spirit. "We didn't give our children any religious training at all," she commented with a note of regret.⁴

August Lowenstein remained observant and chose to be buried with his wife, Marianne, in Cincinnati's Jewish Clifton Cemetery. Their son, David, however, would take his only child Melvyn (Lowenstein's father) to different churches on many Sundays to expose him to a variety of religions—none of which took.

The family's distinguished record in business, by contrast, was more apparent to Lowenstein. His maternal great-grandfather, Edward A. Price, was a dry goods importer in New York who served as a director of several banks. Though he never owned his own company, his more than 50 years as an employee of Frederick Butterfield & Company, where he rose to become senior partner, earned him a handsome living. That was in addition to what his wife, Bertha, had brought to the marriage. Orphaned at a young age, she was raised by a guardian who left her a considerable inheritance.

Together, Edward and Bertha—in need of a vacation home large enough to accommodate their one son and ten daughters—purchased President Ulysses S. Grant's Elberon cottage from his widow, for which they paid $33,000 in 1893.[5] Three stories high with a shingled roof and two glassed-in observatories, the house was a cross between an English villa and a Swiss chalet, as one reporter described it. All of Grant's memorabilia remained on display—an old pine desk used by Grant himself; a plaque of medals honoring his exploits during the Civil War; a small statue depicting Grant, Abraham Lincoln, and Lincoln's war secretary, Edwin Stanton, in a "council of war"; a cabinet presented to Grant by the Dutch government during one of his many post-presidential European tours; and countless family portraits. It was to be the summer home for four generations of the family. It was sold in 1944.[6]

James A. Goldsmith himself was still more successful. As a young man he joined the family business, Hess, Goldsmith & Co., which specialized in silk and rayon products. The firm would eventually be acquired by Burlington Industries, one of the world's largest textile makers. After 15 years working in the company mills outside Wilkes-Barre, Pennsylvania, he moved to New York, where he became president of the company. An industry leader who worked to improve the quality and reliability of Chinese silk supplies and as president of the Silk Manufacturers Association, he led missions for that organization to Egypt, Japan, and China. He also served on the boards of the Chase National Bank (the precursor to J. P. Morgan Chase) and the Equitable Trust Company, as well as the National Industrial Conference Board (now the Conference Board).[7] And he was president of the Harmonic Club from 1918 to 1920.

Lowenstein's father, Melvyn Lowenstein, also earned considerable professional distinction. Raised and educated in Cincinnati, he came to New York City as a naval officer during the First World War and decided to stay. He became a corporate lawyer on Wall Street, representing companies large and small. His specialty was trusts and estates, and he would go on to serve many wealthy families, often serving on the boards of their family firms. He also served on the board of Burlington Industries after it acquired Hess Goldsmith. In the early 1930s, Melvyn joined Wellman, Smyth & Scofield, which found a burgeoning market in helping families restructure their estates to minimize the impact of more progressive New Deal-era taxation. Demand was so great that the firm's business actually increased during the Depression. He soon became a protégé of the senior partner, noted trial attorney Francis L. Wellman, who dedicated his last book to Lowenstein. Wellman was best known for one of his first books, *The Art of Cross Examination* (1903), which influenced generations of trial lawyers and was still an assigned text at Harvard Law School in the mid-1950s, when James Lowenstein was there. Upon Wellman's death in 1942, Melvyn would take over the firm, which changed names several time over the next 30 years.[8]

Melvyn's most famous client was George Herman "Babe" Ruth, the legendary slugger of the New York Yankees. A notorious spendthrift, Ruth had squandered much of his earnings by the time he retired from baseball in 1935. Melvyn was asked to help get Ruth's finances under control by J. Paul Carey, the owner of a Cadillac rental agency and a fellow trustee of The Children's Village, a home for orphans and juvenile delinquents. Melvyn drew up a trust and then he and Carey, as trustees, doled out a monthly allowance to Ruth, who was forever grateful. "Gordon," as Ruth called Melvyn, served as Ruth's attorney for the rest of Ruth's life and was the executor of Ruth's estate. Ruth also made special mention of Melvyn in his autobiography, praising him for giving "the best business advice an easy-come, easy-go guy ever had."[9]

If James Lowenstein was passionate about anything, it was not baseball but the world beyond American shores—an interest he shared with his mother, Katherine.[10] A *cum laude* graduate of Bryn Mawr who spoke some German, French, and Italian and took Spanish lessons in her late nineties, she was a highly cultivated woman with an insatiable appetite for travel.[11] In a poem she delivered at her 95th birthday party, she observed that she had been to 56 countries and had traveled on 26 ships.

Though life in Shrewsbury was pleasant, Melvyn Lowenstein tired of the long commute by train to New York City, and the local schooling options were not very good. In 1937, the family relocated to Scarsdale, in Westchester County, while still spending summers in Elberon. Lowenstein, who adored the country life in Shrewsbury, resented the move from the moment they pulled into the driveway of the new house. Not surprisingly, he was eager to go to boarding school when the time came.

In fall of 1942, Lowenstein enrolled in the Loomis School in Windsor, Connecticut, as a sophomore, but because of his young age he was put in the freshman dorm, where he shared a room with four other boys. One in particular would have a lasting influence. Andrzej (Andy) Beck was the son of the former Polish foreign minister Colonel Józef Beck, who in 1934 had negotiated non-aggression pacts with Germany and the Soviet Union. Listening to Andy's tales of life in prewar Poland with his visits to his family's country chateau, Lowenstein became fascinated with Eastern Europe, even though the world that Andy described had vanished by then. After Germany invaded Poland in 1939, the elder Beck was interned with other members of the Polish government in Romania while his wife and children, including Andy, fled to America. Lowenstein would remember vividly the day in 1944 when he and several of Andy's friends were summoned to the office of the headmaster, who told them bluntly: "We're going to have to tell Andy that his father is dead."

By then, Lowenstein hardly needed a reminder of the world beyond Loomis, for the Second World War had cast a long shadow over life there. Wartime shortages of fuel and rubber curtailed interscholastic sports and discouraged parents from driving to campus to visit their children. With faculty ranks depleted by military enlistments, students took over such duties as monitoring study halls, serving meals, and maintaining the grounds. Many students contributed to the war effort either by raising money or by volunteering their time, while masters provided regular updates on the progress of the war with maps charting the movements of Allied and enemy forces.[12]

The war also altered Loomis's traditional academic program. With a third of the school's regular faculty gone off to war, the headmaster had to scrounge for replacements wherever he could find them. Lowenstein's French teacher, René Cheruy, for example, was the former head of the Loomis French department who had come out of retirement to teach. A former secretary to the sculptor Auguste Rodin, Cheruy had served as an interpreter with British forces in France during the First World War, winning numerous British and French medals for bravery in the field. On the first day of class, Cheruy held up a red book, J. Castaréde's *A Complete Treatise on the Conjugation of French Verbs*. "This little book is going to be your best friend," he said.

Lowenstein said, "Cheruy taught French the way the French taught French. He went around the room with a wooden ruler, and if you made a mistake he rapped you on your knuckles. It was an extremely effective teaching technique." Another of Lowenstein's masters who had come to fill in was William Skenkel Knickerbocker. A former professor of English at the University of the South, where he edited *The Sewanee Review*, Knickerbocker nurtured Lowenstein's interest in writing. Lowenstein made regular contributions to the school yearbook and the literary magazine, and when he left Loomis, he was certain he wanted to be a writer.[13]

Lowenstein was age 16 when he was due to graduate in the spring of 1944. He applied to Yale and Harvard, but both schools advised him to take a post-graduate year at Loomis and enter college with students his own age. Of course, with the end of the war not yet assured despite the D-Day landings of June 6, military service loomed for all able-bodied young men. In his post-graduate year at Loomis, Lowenstein decided to enlist in the US Army Air Corps' Air Cadets, a massive flight-training program that was producing some 66,000 pilots, 16,000 bombardiers, and 16,000 navigators every year. By signing up for the Air Cadets, Lowenstein agreed to accept a commission as a second lieutenant in the US Army Air Corps Reserve two weeks after his 18th birthday and serve three years on active duty at the completion of his training. He received a pair of wings, which he wore every day in his lapel. Then, on August 6, 1945, the day he turned 18, the United States dropped the first atomic bomb on Hiroshima, Japan, and a few days later the second on Nagasaki. Within a matter of days the Air Cadet program was suspended and then cancelled. Lowenstein received an honorable discharge without having served a single day in the military, although he remained eligible for the draft, which was also suspended before he was called up.

The news about Hiroshima had come to Lowenstein at Yale, where he had enrolled in June 1945. He was the twelfth member of his family to attend Yale. The first was Otto M. Goldsmith, class of 1898.[14] In fall of 1945, Yale was just embarking on a major reconversion to peacetime, which brought a massive influx of students. The 900 men who had left for war in the middle of their freshman year were entitled to return, as were the 1,500 who had been admitted to Yale but had never matriculated. Younger students like Lowenstein were arriving directly from secondary school. Soon the GI Bill brought veterans to campus, many of them with families. Add to that the men and women in the graduate programs and professional schools. By September 1946, the start of Lowenstein's sophomore year, there were more than 9,000 students on campus—almost twice the prewar total of 5,000.[15] Yale strained to find beds for everyone. Occupancy was doubled in each of Yale's 10 residential colleges—including Silliman, where Lowenstein was living.[16]

Lowenstein had entered Yale intending to major in English literature. He soon switched to international relations, which seemed more relevant to a world that was fast being remade by the nascent Cold War. He took courses in diplomatic history with Samuel Flagg Bemis, a Pulitzer Prize-winning historian and biographer, courses in international politics with Arnold Wolfers, a Swiss-American lawyer and economist, and a seminar on Eastern Europe. He also enrolled in an intensive course in Russian language to see whether he had any aptitude for it. He didn't, at least not in comparison with the other three students in the class, two with Russian-speaking parents and one with an obvious knack for languages. An introduction to the Cyrillic alphabet would, however, prove useful later in life when Lowenstein needed to learn Serbo-Croatian.[17]

Lowenstein also nurtured his interest in international relations through two summers abroad. The first, in 1947, took him in Mexico City as part of a program organized by the Universidad Nacional de Mexico. He and another student, Howard Berger from Trinity College, were assigned to a host family, Ignacio and Carmen Amor. Though Ignacio had suffered severe financial losses in the worldwide Depression of the 1930s, he remained well connected in Mexico City society and was eager to show the two Americans a Mexico that was different from the one they would find through their Spanish language class at the university. He persuaded them to drop the Spanish language class and he proceeded to introduce them to everyone he knew. "We really integrated into Mexican life," Lowenstein recalled. "The consequence was that we didn't learn much Spanish."

His appetite for international travel now whetted, Lowenstein arranged to spend the following summer in Czechoslovakia through the Experiment in International Living, but those plans were cancelled when the Communists there took power in February 1948. Instead, he went to Sweden and stayed in a village on the shores of Lake Vättern, near Karlsborg, about a three-hour drive from Stockholm. He spent the first month with the Enderlein family, whose son, Thomas, was his age. For the second month, he hiked and cycled all around Sweden in the company of other program participants and their host family siblings.

The summer in Sweden included one memorable event, the result of a serendipitous encounter the previous winter. On several weekend ski trips to Vermont, Lowenstein had befriended a Swede he knew only as Marc, who was then a first-year student at Harvard Business School. When Lowenstein learned he was going to Sweden instead of Czechoslovakia, he telephoned Marc to share the news. "Good," said Marc, "I'll give you a letter to take to my father. He works at a bank. He'll take care of you." Lowenstein took the letter with him, and when he arrived in Stockholm, he marched into the Stockholms Enskilda Bank (now Skandinaviska Enskilda Banken) and asked to see Marc's father. Little did he realize that Marc's father was Marcus "Dodde" Wallenberg, Jr., the CEO of Sweden's most prestigious private bank and the leading member of the family dynasty that had dominated Swedish banking and industry for some 200 years. Lowenstein's youthful innocence became something of a legend in the Wallenberg family, as he discovered years later when he got to know Peter Wallenberg, another of Marcus Wallenberg's sons. "I've heard all about you," Peter said. "You're the only person in the world who didn't have the foggiest idea who we were."[18]

Perhaps the most lasting impression of the summer for Lowenstein was sitting around the radio with his Swedish host family listening to reports of the Berlin airlift—the first major crisis of the emerging Cold War. Lowenstein recalled: "It was impossible to go through those years and not identify with what was going on in the world."

Returning for his final year at Yale, he decided to apply for the Foreign Service. The Rogers Act of 1924, which merged diplomatic and consular services, provided a merit-based career path in the Foreign Service, and the State Department began recruiting Foreign Service officers according to their performance on strenuous written and oral examinations. Eager to begin, Lowenstein skipped his own Yale commencement ceremony in order to begin a two-month Foreign Service preparatory course at George Washington University. He was one of about 50 students in the class who were cramming for the three-and-a-half-day written component, which was heavy on economics and history. For those who passed, returning veterans were given preference for the oral component, which meant that Lowenstein's plan to join the Foreign Service would be temporarily on hold.[19]

Through a friend of his father in the Economic Cooperation Administration (ECA)—the administrative arm of the Marshall Plan, which had been passed into law in April 1948—Lowenstein heard about a management trainee program, to which he applied and was accepted.[20]

Just after the new year in 1950, Lowenstein began packing his bags for the ECA headquarters in Washington. Instead, with ECA officials facing a personnel shortage in Europe, he was re-assigned at the last minute to the European headquarters of the Marshall Plan, called the Office of the Special Representative (OSR). In late January 1950, Lowenstein found himself on a plane bound for Paris.

1 The Marshall Plan

An American in Paris

> To be young, to be American were wonderful things in the late 1940s; to be one of Averell Harriman's aides, or an aide to one of his aides, was transcendental.[21]
>
> Charles L. Mee, Jr., *The Marshall Plan*, p. 249

That was how Lowenstein remembered his time at the European headquarters of the Marshall Plan in Paris. It was to prove to be the adventure of a lifetime, one that transformed Lowenstein as completely as the Marshall Plan itself transformed Europe and its relationship with the United States.

The Marshall Plan came at a decisive moment for the emerging postwar world. Much of the material damage of the war had been repaired with remarkable speed. By 1947, however, the European economy remained at a standstill, which all but doomed prospects for political stability and social reform. The continent suffered widespread food shortages, while a brutal winter, the coldest in living memory, added to a sense of hopelessness. Europe also faced two structural issues.

One was the effective disappearance of Germany from the European economy. Without Germany, no economic recovery could be sustained, as Germany was an industrial powerhouse.

The other was the dollar gap. A lack of economic capacity throughout Europe had left Europeans with nothing to sell, and Europe needed to sell products in order to earn the foreign currency they needed to purchase vital imports.[22] The United States, meanwhile, was locked in an escalating ideological struggle with the Soviet Union. American policymakers knew that continued economic weakness made the appeal of Communism more powerful to a generation of Europeans worn out by the Depression and war, as evidenced by the strength of Communist parties across Europe, and particularly in France and Italy.

Their answer was the Marshall Plan, also known as the European Recovery Program. Announced by US Secretary of State George C. Marshall at Harvard University's commencement on June 5, 1947, and signed into law the following April, the massive economic assistance program was notable for its ingenious distribution mechanism. It furnished dollar credits for the purchase of desperately-needed goods such as food, fuel, flour, wheat, wool, cotton, textiles, tractors, farm and drilling equipment, and aircraft parts. When sold, these goods would then generate additional counterpart funds that recipient countries could invest in reconstruction and rehabilitation and use to defray the costs of administering the program. Thus, unlike the billions of dollars in disaster relief the United States had already committed to Europe, the Marshall Plan had a built-in multiplier effect that Americans hoped would not only stimulate long-term investment but also empower Europeans to resist Communism. Foreign aid, in short, became a way of preserving both democracy and capitalism.

A new government entity, the Economic Cooperation Administration (ECA), and its supervisory arm in Europe, the Office of the Special Representative (OSR), was charged with administering this enterprise. The first US Special

Representative, Averell Harriman, was a Wall Street banker and former ambassador to the Soviet Union and the Court of St. James. When Lowenstein arrived in Paris, Harriman's deputy, the Harvard Law School professor Milton Katz, was in charge of the Marshall Plan.

Lowenstein was, of course, far removed from Harriman and Katz—though perhaps not far enough for Malcolm Pitts, the director of OSR administrative services who was there to greet Lowenstein in the lobby of his Paris hotel. A grizzled veteran of the Civil Service, Pitts bristled at the apparent insouciance of the 22-year-old trainee, standing there with tennis racket slung over his shoulder. Lowenstein was immediately packed off to a Paris warehouse, where his job was to track the inventory and delivery of furniture, machinery, office equipment, and other goods to ECA missions around Europe. What this maiden assignment lacked in glamor it made up for in life lessons, for Lowenstein's boss, George Sinaciawicz, proved to be a master at navigating government bureaucracies. "If you had to be on a desert island, he was the person you would want to have with you," Lowenstein recalled. "He knew how to get anything done—socially, professionally, it didn't make a difference."[23]

After two months in the warehouse, Pitts relented and reassigned Lowenstein to the permanent staff of OSR, where he rotated through various functional areas. These included a stint working in Brussels on the ECA's vast public information program, which churned out films, pamphlets, posters, and exhibitions designed to explain the true purpose of the Marshall Plan and to counter Communist propaganda against the plan. Lowenstein's most rewarding assignment, however, came in the organization and management division of OSR, where he reported to Jack Kubisch. Kubisch was a Navy veteran of the battles of Iwo Jima and Okinawa and had spent a year at Harvard Business School after the war. He schooled Lowenstein in the management principles he had learned at Harvard, and he applied those principles when he allocated OSR's administrative budget to ECA missions. Kubisch was just six years older than Lowenstein, but, like many who had fought in the war, he seemed wise beyond his years. His mature demeanor was reinforced by his discerning attire and homburg. To Lowenstein, he was an almost godlike figure.[24]

Lowenstein's rotations took him from one ECA/OSR office to another, perhaps none more richly symbolic of the American role in Europe than OSR headquarters in the Hôtel de Talleyrand, one of the grandest mansions in Paris and a masterpiece of French Enlightenment architecture. There, on the third floor, hundreds of Americans toiled away in a warren of small cubicles, many with electrical and telephone wires trailing along the floor. Space was at a premium, leaving some secretaries to work out of bathrooms, their typewriters perched on bidets.[25] The heating system frequently broke down. In the winter months, an aide often brought in wood to light a fire in one of the ornate marble fireplaces. "Even if it doesn't keep them warm, it will cheer them up," Pitts's predecessor William J. Sheppard liked to say."[26]

The Marshall Planners, 3,000 of which were in Paris, were a mix of university economists, government officials, and young aides like Lowenstein. Smart, hard-working, and dedicated, they reveled in the idealism of public service in the aftermath of a world war. Twelve-hour days and six-day weeks were commonplace. The Marshall Planners brought a distinct can-do spirit to their work. In contrast to the lofty economic and social plans that lacked specifics in postwar Europe, the Marshall Plan set out a framework and urged Europeans to make it work, knowing that American involvement would be short-lived. "We were constantly plotting how to get something done and who should do it," recalled Roger Fisher, a Harvard law professor who had worked under Harriman in 1948 and 1949. Lowenstein echoed this impression. The staffs of both OSR and the ECA missions to France, he recalled later, were the most competent group of people he had ever encountered. "There was no gossip, no protocol, and very little jockeying for power. I never ran into anyone who didn't know what he was doing…. everyone was dedicated to getting things done."[27]

Despite their long hours, the Marshall Planners were also eager to enjoy themselves. "The boys had all been through the war," wrote a secretary at the US embassy in Paris, "and felt cheated of a knowledge of life. Before settling down to an executive desk, they wanted to savor a taste of something they might never have again."[28] Though Lowenstein was too young to have fought in the war, he too made time to enjoy what Paris had to offer. He socialized after hours with other Americans in Paris, befriending three in particular: Frederic L. Chapin, an economic analyst with OSR; Arthur Hartman, who had dropped out of Harvard Law School to join the ECA mission to France; and John W. Barnum, a Yale classmate who was working for an American brokerage firm.

Lowenstein was also determined to experience everyday French life. Early on, he took lodgings with a French family—a mother and her two teenaged children—who let him a room in their apartment in Rue Theodore de Banville in the 17th arrondissement. Perhaps eager for the rental income, the mother promised Lowenstein that he could expect to meet the famous Alice Joséphine "Lily" Pons, a French-American operatic soprano, who the mother said came for tea on Sundays. Not so, he learned a few weeks after moving in. "Young man," an elderly resident of the building told him in the elevator, "Lily Pons came for tea once four years ago. She's never coming back."[29]

Lowenstein mixed easily with the French. His burgeoning social circle owed much to a weekend house party he attended in the Normandy fishing port of Dieppe not long after he arrived. There he met a young Frenchman who introduced himself as Pierre, and the two shared a ride back to Paris. Lowenstein discovered later that his new acquaintance was Baron Pierre de Gunzburg, the 20-year-old scion of a wealthy Russian-Jewish family that had made its fortune in banking and oil in Czarist Russia. The family fled to France during the Russian Revolution. After the fall of France to the Germans in 1940, they fled again, this time to the United States. When Pierre and his family returned to Paris sometime in the late

1940s, they were naturally predisposed to like Americans like Lowenstein. "Every American was a friend by nature," recalled Pierre's son, Vivien.[30] Besides introducing Lowenstein to his family and friends, Pierre helped Lowenstein find a new apartment in a building owned by another French noble, Baroness de Ladoucette. Located at 172 Rue de l'Université in the seventh arrondissement near the Pont de l'Alma and the Pont des Invalides, it was a considerable upgrade. It was also the first of many situations early in Lowenstein's career that would lead to connections later in life. Many years on, when he was working as a consultant, Lowenstein was invited to a meeting of the International Advisory Board of ELF Aquitaine, the French oil company (now Total), whose secretary was none other than Vera de Ladoucette, a relative of Baroness de Ladoucette by marriage.[31] Lowenstein and Pierre, meanwhile, would remain lifelong friends, visiting with each other's families and socializing at their Paris club, the Travellers.

Such a vibrant social life was possible in part because Lowenstein, like other American expatriates in Paris, could afford to live well. He had only an entry-level position in a government job, but as a Foreign Service Staff (FSS) Class 12, his starting annual salary was $3,200, which, after the franc was devalued against the dollar in 1948, went a long way. Hard currency enabled Lowenstein to live in relative luxury on a housing allowance of $86 a month. He bought a Renault 4 for the equivalent of $500, which allowed him to get out of Paris and see the French countryside and even something of Spain. He joined a tennis club, the Racing Club de France in the Bois de Boulogne. And he made sure that he was at the Stade Roland-Garros for the 1950 French Championships, where he watched the American tennis ace Tony Trabert win the men's doubles title.

If Americans like Lowenstein enjoyed Paris, not all Parisians enjoyed Americans. As recipients of American aid, Europeans felt an uneasy mixture of gratitude and resentment toward their benefactors. While Americans were generally appreciated across Europe, they were also "in varying degrees, hated, disliked, mistrusted, or accepted either in humiliation or restraint," according to American journalist Theodore White.[32] This was especially true in France, where many on the political left regarded the small, elite group of Americans with suspicion—agents of a new dollar dictatorship. Lowenstein saw this for himself in the anti-American slogans plastered on buildings all around Paris: "Les Americains en Amerique" and "Ami Go Home." To the latter, Lowenstein's friend Clem Brown, an employee of an American airline, always added "Via Pan American."[33]

Probing his French friends for insight, Lowenstein came to see that French anti-American feelings had as much to do with the French themselves as with Americans. By 1950, France was already mired in a colonial war in southeast Asia, which despite massive US military assistance, was not going well. Its politics were notoriously dysfunctional, the result of a weak presidency and a vigorous Communist party. France had no fewer than five prime ministers during Lowenstein's first 18 months in Europe, including Henri Queuille, whose second ministry in July 1950 lasted a mere 10 days.

Above all, there was the stain of wartime collaboration. Though many European nations grappled with this bitter legacy, it was particularly pronounced in France, which had endured both the German occupation and its own Vichy regime. Some 6,800 collaborators were sentenced to death between 1944 and 1951, with nearly 800 of those sentences carried out. Another 50,000 were sentenced to national degradation, which barred them from most business fiduciary and ownership positions as well as whole professions, like teaching. Others received more modest punishments. In all, the purge directly touched some 350,000 people in France.[34] Memories of collaboration died hard. Lowenstein said, "I remember walking with a friend's father who crossed the street to avoid greeting a man he knew well but who had been a Vichy collaborator." Lowenstein found the case of Jean Borotra especially compelling.[35] One of the Four Musketeers—the top tennis players during the interwar years—Borotra had served briefly as the commissioner of general education and sport in the French Vichy government. Though he was later taken prisoner while trying to join Allied forces in North Africa, his role in the Vichy regime remained a source of controversy all his life. Lowenstein would later meet Borotra on the tennis court. In 1972, the two competed in a doubles match in a 45 and over tournament held in the second week of the French championships at Roland Garros. "You don't look old enough to play in this tournament," Borotra said to Lowenstein. "I was born in 1927," Lowenstein replied. "Ah, 1927," said Borotra, "the year I was a finalist at Forest Hills."

An American in Sarajevo

One morning in June 1950, as Lowenstein was eating breakfast at his usual Paris café, he heard radio reports that North Korean troops had invaded South Korea, signaling the start of the Korean War. His first thought was: "This is going to mean military service." Lowenstein decided not to wait to be drafted. Instead, he flew back to the United States to apply for naval officer candidate school, following in the footsteps of his father, a naval officer in the First World War. Then he returned to Paris and waited to be called up.[36]

That fall, Lowenstein declined an offer to serve as an administrative officer in the ECA mission in Iceland, deciding to remain in Paris until his number came up with the Navy. Then, on a Thursday afternoon in early December, he received a telephone call from the OSR personnel office with a new assignment: he would be joining the US Special Mission to Yugoslavia to help administer the American famine relief program that was signed into law just days earlier.[37]

Again, Lowenstein demurred. He was happy in Paris, he explained, and in any case he expected to be summoned soon to officer candidate school. A few hours later, he received another call, this one from Everett H. Bellows, a senior official.[38] "This is not a request; it's an order," he said. If Lowenstein still did not want to go, Bellows added, then he could forget about a career in the Foreign Service. So on Saturday at 5 o'clock in the afternoon, Lowenstein found himself aboard the Orient Express bound for Yugoslavia.[39]

The US Special Mission to Yugoslavia, though nominally separate from the Marshall Plan, was driven by the same Cold War logic. Yugoslavia was one of six European countries to have refused participation in the Marshall Plan, having been ordered to do so by Stalin. After Yugoslavia's leader, Marshal Josip Broz (Tito), was expelled from the Cominform in June 1948, George Kennan—a master strategist and author of the American containment strategy—saw a chance to drive a wedge between the Soviet Union and Yugoslavia through a program of trade.[40] This was American policy when, in 1950, a devastating drought hit Yugoslavia, causing large-scale crop failures. The resulting food crisis, exacerbated by Tito's rigid collectivism, produced shortfalls of an estimated one million tons of corn and half a million tons of wheat. In October, Tito's government appealed to Ambassador George V. Allen for emergency food assistance.[41]

The State Department responded with a major famine relief plan for Yugoslavia. The proposal encountered stiff resistance in Congress, where some members still found it hard to reconcile even humanitarian aid with hardline anti-Communism. But President Harry S. Truman's administration lobbied hard. Even Allen weighed in, showing to holdouts on Capitol Hill the movies he had taken in hard-hit regions. Finally, in December 1950, Congress approved a $38 million aid plan on the condition that American observers be allowed into the country to monitor distribution.[42]

Richard F. Allen was tapped to lead the monitoring team. A former vice chairman of the American Red Cross,[43] Allen quickly assembled a team of experienced humanitarian aid officers from the United Nations Relief and Rehabilitation Administration (UNRRA), which had provided disaster relief and helped repatriate legions of postwar refugees, and supplemented them with personnel from the Foreign Service and the ECA. Lowenstein was drafted as a last-minute replacement for one member who had died of a heart attack during briefings in Paris. "Allen must have called Bellows and said he needed a body," Lowenstein surmised. "I suspect he said that any body would do, and I also suspect that Bellows didn't spend a lot of time looking. Hence the telephone call." As it happened, John A. Baker, Jr., Lowenstein's Loomis and Yale classmate and a junior officer in the political section of the US embassy in Belgrade, would later volunteer to become an observer in Macedonia after a second member of the mission died suddenly.[44]

Lowenstein and his fellow aid observers disembarked in Trieste, then an independent state under the protection of US and British forces. They received briefings and were outfitted with jeeps, winter outer clothing, and C-rations. A week later, Lowenstein and the others set off on the drive through mountain roads to Zagreb, the capital of Croatia, where they were to receive further briefings. They didn't make it even as far as Ljubljana, a halfway point, before their jeeps stalled in snow drifts and needed to be hauled out by horses.[45]

At last, sometime in early December, the observers began to fan out across Yugoslavia to each of its six republics. Other members of the mission had claimed the plum assignments for themselves, leaving Lowenstein, a late arrival, with Bosnia-Herzegovina, which was isolated, mountainous, and poor. Lowenstein packed up his jeep, hooked up a trailer filled with C-rations and two spare tires, and headed for Sarajevo, the capital of Bosnia-Herzegovina. The journey took 12 hours. Heavy snow and biting cold made for slow going. Lowenstein had no command of the Serbo-Croatian language, so the Cyrillic road signs were of little help, and he couldn't ask for directions except to point left or right and say "Sarajevo?" By the time he arrived in the Bosnian capital, he was as close to exhaustion as he had ever been.[46]

For the next seven months, Lowenstein visited every municipality in the republic of Bosnia-Herzegovina to observe the distribution of American foodstuffs. Traveling with an interpreter, he was on the road Monday through Saturday, from six in the morning until dusk. It was tiring work, although straightforward. Lowenstein drove to the main aid distribution points, where he stopped people on the street to ask whether they had received the food that was promised to them and whether they had observed any corruption. "It didn't take a genius to figure out how to do this," he said.[47]

It did, however, require tact and persistence. American aid observers were at the mercy of their interpreters for what information they could gather. Lowenstein's interpreter was a graduate student from Belgrade in Serbia, and his scarcely-concealed contempt for those in the hinterlands of Bosnia-Herzegovina was doubtless met in kind. Neither he nor any interpreter was likely to be taken into the confidence of the person on the street, as the interpreters were Yugoslav nationals employed by a foreign embassy. The government discouraged the common people from fraternizing with foreigners.[48] As Baker recalled of his own interpreter in Macedonia later that year, "It was quite clear that the people being interviewed didn't quite trust the interpreter…I wasn't quite sure I trusted her either." Yet if observers were therefore limited in what they could learn, this did not make their role any less important. "We were pretending to observe much more than in fact we were capable of observing," Lowenstein conceded. "But the observing we did do was a deterrent to abuses."[49]

Lowenstein also had to contend with a Communist government that was unaccustomed to foreigners operating in its midst. While some food aid observers credited Yugoslav officials with full cooperation, this cooperation was not universal. Party apparatchiks in Macedonia, for example, were clearly unhappy to be on the American dole and did little to spread the word about American aid.[50] Lowenstein was fortunate that the party boss in Bosnia-Herzegovina, a Bosnian Croat named Rudi Kolak, had thrown his weight behind the American food aid. But in all their dealings, he was somewhat prickly, his pride wounded by the fact that someone of Lowenstein's relative youth and inexperience had been assigned to his republic.

The official suspicion of foreigners was shown by the fact that two government liaison officers had been assigned to keep an eye on Lowenstein. One was a Bosnian Serb, the other a Bosnian Jew named Albert Finci, who came from an old Sephardic Jewish family. Serbs and Jews, of course, had both suffered grievously during the Second World War at the hands of the Ustaše, the Croatian fascist group that by used Nazi race theory to commit widespread genocide. Of 14,000 Jews in Bosnia before the war, including 12,000 in Sarajevo, just 2,000 remained after the war. Though Lowenstein dined with the two men every other week, he could extract nothing from either of them about their wartime experiences. This had less to do with official reticence, Lowenstein surmised, than with an understandable desire to turn the page on a dark chapter in Yugoslavia's past, one that made Tito's nationalist regime broadly popular.[51]

The aid observers were required to file periodic progress reports with the mission office in Belgrade. Lowenstein's reports went far beyond describing the distribution of American food aid. He included studies of the internal politics of Yugoslavia, synopses of overheard conversations, analyses of social and economic conditions, and summaries of local views on the Communist party and its apparatchiks. "I don't know if anybody ever read these things," he said, "and I don't know what happened to them, but I enjoyed writing them."[52] Indeed, the study of a country's internal political affairs would become a specialty of Lowenstein's future overseas assignments.

Every other month, the aid observers traveled to the US embassy in Belgrade for two or three days of consultations. Belgrade in 1951 was a study in contrasts. A massive building project—*Novi Beograd*, or New Belgrade—was underway. Situated on the west bank of the Sava River, opposite the Old Town, this collection of Modernist towers and high-rises designed in the rough and unadorned Brutalist architectural style was an exercise in socialist urban planning. It was intended to symbolize of the brave new Yugoslavia that Tito aspired to build. The city nevertheless retained some of its old-fashioned touches. On one winter occasion, for example, Lowenstein went from the station to the embassy in a horse-drawn sleigh. It was in Belgrade that he got to know the US ambassador, George V. Allen. Though businesslike in his dealings with subordinates, Allen was also highly sociable. He invited Lowenstein and his fellow observers to dinner whenever they were in Belgrade, and he made a point of visiting each of them in the Yugoslav republics.[53]

For Lowenstein, the occasional trips to Belgrade, as well as visits from Allen and John Baker, were a welcome diversion from life in Sarajevo, which he found bleak and lonely. Home was the Hotel Europa, whose glamor had long since faded. Opened in 1882, the Hotel Europa was Sarajevo's first modern hotel. Service deteriorated, however, after it was nationalized with the Communist takeover in 1945. There was also a constant reminder of Sarajevo's unfortunate place in history. From his bedroom window in the presidential suite, Lowenstein could look out on the street corner where Gavrilo Princip had shot the Serbian Archduke Franz Ferdinand at point blank range in 1914, setting in motion events that led to the First World War. Thirty years later, during the next world war, Dušan Jeftanović, the hotel founder's son and owner of the Hotel Europa, was executed by the Ustaše along with other prominent Serbs from Sarajevo.

Sarajevo, moreover, did not enjoy the vibrant expatriate community that Paris had. Lowenstein did not know of any other foreigners living in Bosnia-Herzegovina. The most recent previous foreigner, to his knowledge, was the Italian consul, Marcello Cavalletti di Oliveti Sabino, who had left Sarajevo with his pregnant wife during the war. Lowenstein would eventually meet Cavalletti in Luxembourg in the late 1970s, when Cavalletti and Lowenstein were serving as the Italian and US ambassadors, respectively.[54]

Eager for diversion, Lowenstein befriended the hotel manager's 19-year-old son, and together they listened to

American jazz on Lowenstein's shortwave radio. But these soirees came to an end after the fellow was warned not to socialize with Americans. Lowenstein also became a devotee of the opera. "I went to the opera several times a week," he said. "I must have seen *Prince Igor* 10 times."[55]

Despite the challenges of dealing with Yugoslav officialdom and the cloistered life of Sarajevo, Lowenstein came to admire the Yugoslavs he did get to know. "I like the life in one way," he told a journalist at the time. "The Bosnians are close-mouthed and it's hard to get to know them, but they've been honest with me."[56] Lowenstein could also take satisfaction in the work he was doing. The United States government judged the famine relief program a great success. Not only did it alleviate hunger in the short term, even within the limits of Yugoslavia's collectivized system, it also helped to improve US-Yugoslav relations, with both governments clearly determined to overcome their mutual suspicions and make their partnership work.[57] Perhaps most important, the aid program accustomed ordinary Yugoslavs to viewing Americans as helpful and non-threatening. As Lowenstein roamed the Bosnian countryside in a US government jeep with an American flag on its fender and "Americki Pomoćni Program Hrane" (American Food Aid) emblazoned on its side, he left no doubt who was responsible for life-saving assistance. One aid observer recalled the gratitude of the Yugoslav people: "I wish I'd counted the number of middle-aged and elderly women who came up to us and patted our hands or cheeks and said how happy they were to see Americans. This happened everywhere…."[58] Lowenstein met with a similar reception. Wherever he went, people gathered around him and peppered him with questions, asking "where I was from, what was I doing there, what more help could America provide, and, inevitably, did I know their cousin in Chicago?"[59]

The Three Wise Men

In June 1951, after seven months in Sarajevo, Lowenstein received notice that he should report to Navy officer candidate school the following January. But before he left Europe, he had one more posting that brought him into close contact with the policy and policymakers of the emerging Atlantic world. That posting returned him to the Hôtel Talleyrand in Paris, where he served as one of two staff aides on the US delegation to the Temporary Council Committee (TCC) of NATO. The other staff aide was Fred Chapin, his friend from OSR.

The TCC had been established in response to a problem that bedevils the NATO alliance to this day: the equitable distribution of defense spending among member nations. In 1951, projections of total force commitments over the next four years—infantry, combat aircraft, warships and submarines, ordnance, and support equipment and personnel—remained far below what was needed for the collective defense of Western Europe. But as economic recovery slowly began to take hold, Europeans were reluctant to accede to American demands for more resources, especially at a time when the imminent threat of Soviet military action appeared to be diminishing.[60] After a meeting in Ottawa failed to resolve the impasse, NATO delegates appointed a steering committee, the TCC, to come up with a formula for determining European defense commitments, much as the Organization for European Economic Cooperation (OEEC) had done in helping to apportion Marshall Plan aid.

The TCC consisted of three men who were dubbed the Wise Men: Averell Harriman, who had returned to Paris expressly for the purpose; Jean Monnet, the father of the European Coal and Steel Community; and British industrialist and government adviser Sir Edwin Plowden. They had very able assistants whom Harriman recruited from OSR, including Lincoln Gordon, vice chairman of the War Production Board during the war and later ambassador to Brazil and eventually president of Johns Hopkins; Henry J. Tasca, who would go on to serve as ambassador to Greece and Morocco; Colonel Charles H. Bonesteel, the future commanding general of the Eighth Army; and George A. Lincoln, the principal planner for US military campaigns under General George C. Marshall and who would later head the Policy Planning Staff of the State Department.

Still, even talent of this high order could not close the gap between the needs of collective European security on the one hand and the economic and political limitations of European members on the other. In the end, Harriman, Monnet, and Plowden fudged it, setting bold goals for commitments of armed forces but making the fulfillment of those commitments flexible. They also recommended strengthening NATO's infrastructure with headquarters facilities, communications networks, air bases, munitions depots, and transport. These recommendations were endorsed at the NATO summit in Lisbon in February 1952. This infrastructure, Lincoln Gordon noted, gave NATO "sufficient institutional substance to carry it through its dangerous infancy." Thus, even as they left the issue of equitable assignment of contributions to become a permanent source of friction between the United States and its NATO allies, they helped transform NATO from a mutual defense treaty into a formidable military organization with the United States at its heart.[61]

Lowenstein described his role in these negotiations as that of a glorified messenger boy. Together with Fred Chapin, he arranged calendars, proofread memos, and collated papers. "But if you're going to do this kind of thing," he said, "it might as well be for Harriman, Monnet, and Plowden and at a desk overlooking the Place de la Concorde." The arrangement made Lowenstein privy to conversations about US troop levels and burden-sharing that were fundamental to the Atlantic alliance, and what he learned at the side of the Wise Men would later prove invaluable when, as a Senate Foreign Relations Committee staff member, he analyzed issues related to Mutual Balanced Force Reductions negotiations with the Warsaw Pact. The relationship with Monnet, in particular, lasted for many years. When Lowenstein visited Paris as Deputy Assistant

Secretary for European Affairs in the mid-1970s, he and Arthur Hartman, the Assistant Secretary, would often call on Monnet at his apartment on Avenue Foch.[62]

The Marshall Plan and two of its offshoots, the US Special Mission to Yugoslavia and NATO, involved Lowenstein in three enterprises of significant importance, both for the postwar world and for his own life and work.

First was the Marshall Plan. In three and a half short years, from April 1948, when it was enacted, until December 1951, when it ended, the United States had transferred nearly $13.2 billion to 16 European countries, or fully 5.4 percent of US GDP in 1948 dollars—greater than the sum of all previous US overseas aid combined. Its impact exceeded its scale. By one estimate, industrial output in the Marshall Plan countries increased by an average of 60 percent between 1947 and 1952, with large gains in Sweden (211 percent) and Germany (241 percent). This was a huge increase compared to the growth rate of the 27 European Union countries between 2003 and 2008, which was 15 percent. The Marshall Plan growth rates were 2 to 5 percentage points higher than they would have been without Marshall Plan aid. For the architects of the Marshall Plan, however, the real goal was a symbolic one. It was the long-term commitment of the United States to European security. That was more important than stimulating the economy.[63]

The Marshall Plan also helped spur European integration. Though it left the details of purchases largely to the countries themselves, the plan nudged governments to coordinate with each other to determine how the funds were invested—most notably through the instruments of the Organization for European Economic Cooperation (OEEC) and the European Payments Union, which facilitated multilateral trade and international settlements.[65] By also making possible the reintegration of Germany into the European economy, the Marshall Plan encouraged France to believe it was safer as part of an integrated Europe, and that hastened the realization of Monnet's vision of a united Europe.[66] The Plan eventually led to the formation of the European Union and the single European currency.

Security was also the main objective of the food aid to Yugoslavia, which Lowenstein recognized as a stroke of political genius. Indeed, the goodwill it generated, combined with the closer ties between Washington and Belgrade that it necessitated, set the stage for a larger policy of economic and later military assistance whose goal was, according to R. Borden Reams, *chargé d'affaires* in Belgrade, to keep Tito afloat. Over the next decade, the United States would commit some $1.5 billion in such aid to Yugoslavia.[64] While this policy never succeeded in enticing Tito into the Western alliance, it was critical in allowing him to remain independent of Moscow.

The formation of NATO rested on the realization that there could be no economic security in Europe without physical security. This became all too apparent after the Soviets and their Eastern European satellites rejected Marshall Plan aid, thus hardening the division of Europe.

Finally, these early years in Europe led to later opportunities for Lowenstein. An acquaintance in the senior ranks of the ECA mission to France was responsible for his first assignment in the Foreign Service. Lowenstein's experience in Yugoslavia would lead to his assignment at the Belgrade embassy a decade later. When fellow Marshall Planner Arthur Hartman rose to become Assistant Secretary of State for European Affairs in 1974, he would invite Lowenstein to join him as a Deputy Assistant Secretary. And the nearly two years in Paris helped Lowenstein form a lifelong attachment to France.

2 From the Navy to the Foreign Service

The Navy

In January 1952, Lowenstein reported to Newport, Rhode Island, naval base for the start of officer candidate school. The training lasted 16 weeks and covered all that one would expect the officer class of a modern navy to know: seamanship, navigation, command structure, engineering, weapons, and military law. Of these, navigation was the only real challenge for Lowenstein, who lacked a head for numbers.[67]

At the end of his training, Lowenstein was commissioned as an ensign. He had always hoped to serve on a big ship, and he got his wish with his first assignment: the USS *Coral Sea*. A 45,000-ton Midway-class aircraft carrier with 130 aircraft and 4,500 officers and sailors, the *Coral Sea* was one of the three largest carriers in the US fleet. The *Midway* and the *Franklin D. Roosevelt* were the others.

The *Coral Sea* was the flagship of Carrier Division Six and it patrolled the Mediterranean as part of the US Navy's Sixth Fleet, which was headquartered in Villefranche. Lowenstein, however, had been ordered to join the *Coral Sea* "in whatever port she may be." Absent any further details, he reported to the air base at Windsor Locks, Connecticut (now Bradley Air National Guard Base) to await instruction. He had been there about a week when he was rudely awakened in the middle of the night by two sailors at his door: "You're leaving. Report to Gate A immediately."

Then came a bureaucratic snafu. Lowenstein had been told he was boarding a plane bound for Morocco. The young ensign's seatmate on the flight, a US Army colonel, set him straight. "Why do you keep talking to me about Morocco?" he complained. "This plane is going to Frankfurt. Furthermore, how did you get on this flight? It's for field officers and above."[68]

When he landed in Frankfurt the following day, a Friday, Lowenstein did as he was trained to do when arriving alone in any new city: he reported to the senior officer present. The US Navy liaison desk at the airport told him that the *Coral Sea* was now docked in Naples but that he would have to wait until Monday to be transferred there. With a weekend to spare, he looked up Bill Willis, one of his closest friends from Yale. Willis and another Yale classmate, Gates Davison, had recently been plucked from a US Army psychological warfare unit in Heidelberg and assigned as guards for John J. McCloy, the US High Commissioner for Germany and a close friend of Davison's father, F. Trubee Davison. As military governor, McCloy wielded almost dictatorial power over the lives of ordinary Germans. He was also an icon of the American establishment: Wall Street lawyer, presidential advisor, former president of the World Bank, and confidante of businessmen, philanthropists, and politicians. And yet there, on Saturday night, were Willis, Davison, and Lowenstein—two Army privates with matching MG roadsters and a Navy ensign fresh out of Officer Candidate School—dining with McCloy and his wife, Ellen. The next day, Lowenstein flew to Rome, where again he reported to the senior officer present, who was the chaplain of the *Coral Sea*. Lowenstein tagged along on the chaplain's tour of the Vatican and saw Pope Pius XII hold mass. From there, he boarded the train to Naples to join the *Coral Sea*.[69]

Once aboard, Lowenstein was designated a division officer for air operations, the unit with responsibility for the safe launch and recovery of aircraft from the carrier flight deck. Lowenstein reviewed the personnel list on his first night aboard the ship and saw that one of the 32 sailors under his command was listed as Trabert, T., Seaman 2nd class. The following morning, he found that it was indeed Tony Trabert, the American tennis star whom he had seen play at Roland Garros. Trabert would go on to win the US Open twice, the French Open twice, and Wimbledon once. For now, though, Trabert was a Navy seaman, and it fell to Lowenstein, as his commanding officer, to draft a radiogram to the Secretary of the Navy requesting leave for Trabert to compete at Wimbledon, which was due to begin on June 23. Lowenstein's message went up the chain of command as far as Vice Admiral Lynde McCormick, Commander in Chief of the Sixth Fleet, who denied the request. In the middle of the Korean War, McCormick must have reasoned, it would just not do to have a Navy seaman running around the Wimbledon grass courts in tennis whites surrounded by ladies sipping Pimm's Cups. That did not prevent McCormick from asking Trabert for two tickets to the US Open after Trabert had been posted to the United States later that year, nor Trabert from complying. "What do you think a seaman second class does when an Admiral asks him for something?" Trabert told Lowenstein many years later.[70]

In addition to managing air operations, Lowenstein worked with an intelligence officer on targeting nuclear weapons. Two years earlier, the *Coral Sea* had become the first carrier to launch an aircraft carrying such devastating ordnance.[71] By the time Lowenstein arrived as an ensign on the ship, the presence of nuclear weapons aboard the *Coral Sea* was an open secret throughout the crew. He was also assigned odd jobs that career officers preferred not to do themselves.

Perhaps Lowenstein's oddest job came just a few days after he arrived on the *Coral Sea*. In September 1952, the *Coral Sea* would be docking in Split, Yugoslavia,—the first US ship to dock in Yugoslavia since the end of the war. The stop had been orchestrated to demonstrate to the Soviets that US military aid was both available and acceptable to Yugoslavia. Once again, Lowenstein found himself in close proximity to those in power. Marshal Tito would be boarding the ship, and Lowenstein was ordered to assist senior officers in organizing the details of a day-long cruise with Tito. When Tito and US Ambassador George V. Allen made their way up the gangway, the ship's officers and sailors in dress whites stood on the flight deck. Lowenstein lined up with Rear Admiral Charles Randall "Cat" Brown, Brown's staff, the *Coral Sea*'s captain, and the executive officer. When Ambassador Allen spotted Lowenstein, he said, "Jim, what are you doing here?" He immediately introduced Lowenstein to Tito as "the young man who helped save your country," to which Tito nodded, "Yes, I know, I know."[72]

After a review of officers and men standing at attention on the flight deck, Tito went on to visit every corner of the mammoth ship, stopping just long enough to devour hot dogs in the chow line of the enlisted men's mess hall. Lowenstein, Ambassador Allen, and the Navy brass were with him at every turn.

After Tito departed, the Admiral's aide visited Lowenstein in his cabin. "You know who the other officers in the welcoming party were?" Lowenstein said yes, repeating their names and ranks. "Well, how many times do you think you saluted in the course of the day?" Lowenstein was advised, not so politely, to learn the Navy's saluting protocol in a hurry.

The officers of the *Coral Sea* felt a strong sense of duty toward the sailors in their charge. "Our job as officers," Lowenstein said, "was not to make all these sailors subservient to us, but to make them better citizens. I found that attitude a lot in the Navy."[73] President Truman had announced the formal end of racial segregation in the armed forces in July 1948. After that, the Navy, like the other branches of the armed forces, had become a true engine of social advancement. The *Coral Sea* received its first Black officer while Lowenstein was aboard. Before the officer arrived, the executive officer summoned the other officers to a meeting and announced that he did not want any trouble. There was none. Lowenstein had been told this was the first time a Black officer had been assigned to a major combatant ship since the Navy began to commission Black officers in 1944.[74]

On Lowenstein's second tour with the *Coral Sea*, he served as an interpreter for Rear Admiral Grover Budd Hartley Hall when the ship called on French-speaking ports and the French Foreign Legion headquarters in Sidi Bel Abbès in Algeria. Hall was at that time commander of Carrier Division 6. Lowenstein also acted as the ship's ersatz public affairs officer, cobbling together a ship newspaper based on wire service reports.[75]

After two tours and 18 months aboard the *Coral Sea*, Lowenstein, who was now a Lieutenant junior grade, headed back to Newport, Rhode Island, to join the staff of the Naval War College. A positive comment by Admiral Hall in Lowenstein's personnel file had caught the eye of Robert W. Tucker, a Naval Academy graduate and an international law section junior officer who had been recalled to active duty. Tucker was now scheduled to return to the University of California Berkeley, where he was an assistant professor, and he was looking for a replacement. Lowenstein, with a Yale degree and overseas experience, seemed like a good candidate.

The two had never met before. When they did, Tucker gave Lowenstein a baleful look and took two weighty volumes on international law, one by L. F. L. Oppenheim and the other by Sir Hersch Lauterpacht, and pushed them across the desk. "Lieutenant," he said, "go into that office across the hall and read these books." At some 1,500 pages, Lowenstein could barely lift them.[76] During the following week, Tucker hardly spoke to Lowenstein, until Lowenstein insisted to Tucker that if he were to replace him, they needed to develop a reasonable relationship. The two men started communicating and subsequently became lifelong friends.

Then as now, the Naval War College educated both military and civilian leaders in warfare, strategy, operations, and related disciplines. International law formed a small but important part of this mission. All resident students received one week of instruction in the subject, which was woven into related coursework such as operations.[77] The College also offered a separate correspondence course in international law that Lowenstein administered, marking papers and making adjustments to the curriculum.

Lowenstein's chief duty, however, was to provide research and editorial assistance to a visiting civilian professor named Hans Kelsen. A renowned legal theorist, Kelsen had published numerous works of scholarship over his career, including *Reine Rechtslehre* (*Pure Theory of Law*), which advanced a vision of the law as untainted by political ideology, moral philosophy, or social science. He had also written the Austrian constitution and served as a judge on the Austrian Supreme Constitutional Court. However, as a Jew, Kelsen had been forced out of his university post in Germany in 1933 after the Nazis seized power. He later immigrated to the United States, where he went on to teach at Harvard and the University of California, Berkeley. Kelsen had recently retired from UC Berkeley when Tucker, who had been one of his PhD students there, arranged a one-year appointment for him at the War College.[78]

Kelsen could be coldly logical, A few days after they met, while Lowenstein was studying in the library, Kelsen approached him with a wide grin. "Professor Kelsen, why are you smiling at me that way?" Lowenstein asked. "I always smile when I see a young, healthy, happy boy," Kelsen replied. "Well, how do you know I'm a happy boy?" Lowenstein responded. Kelsen answered, "That you are young is evident. That you are healthy is also evident. That you are happy is an inescapable conclusion in view of the aforementioned two factors." The two would prove to be effective collaborators. Lowenstein was helpful to the German-speaking Kelsen, whose English sentences seemed to run to two pages and were in dire need of editing. The book they worked on together, *Collective Security under International Law*, was published in 1955 as part of a long-running Naval War College series. While the volume remained "hard reading in places," according to one reviewer, Kelsen had made an acute analysis of a fundamental principle:

that collective security, at one time restricted to treaties, had become an essential function of international law.[79]

Most of staff of the Naval War College were older career officers, and most of them were married, living off-base in rented houses. Lowenstein and the other unmarried officers were housed in the cramped Bachelor Officers' Quarters. A few weeks in, Lowenstein decided to try to upgrade his accommodations. "Young naval officer with claustrophobia seeks lodging in a gatehouse of large private mansion," read the tongue-in-cheek ad he placed in the local Newport newspaper. He received a telephone call from Lillian Newlin Van Rensselaer, a wealthy widow who spent her winters in Palm Beach. She owned a sprawling, Italianate mansion on Bellevue Avenue called The Hedges. "My house has 25 rooms," she said to him. "Is that big enough for you?" Unbeknownst to Lowenstein, Van Rensselaer had gained nationwide attention with a series of bitter court battles against Timmy "the Woodhooker" Sullivan—better known as "Timmy the hermit"—and his sister Julia Sullivan, neighbors whose wood piles obscured the entrance to The Hedges. The matter was resolved when Mrs. Van Rensselaer's paid for a fence to surround the Sullivan property.

Lowenstein lived in the caretaker's apartment on the ground floor of The Hedges while Van Rensselaer was in Florida. After nine months of living there, he grew tired of returning home to find the furnace on the fritz, and so he rented an apartment for the remainder of his time in Newport.[80]

Working at the Naval War College proved to be a good way for Lowenstein to serve out the remaining months of his military commitment. He had full run of the College, with its libraries, lectures, and seminars. He received a grounding in international law that was not only fascinating but also an ideal preparation for the ambitious investigative studies he would undertake later in his career. And despite being a junior reserve officer, he felt very well treated by the senior officers. When he eventually departed the Naval War College and married, the officers gave him an engraved silver cigarette box as a wedding present.

A Law School Experiment

Lowenstein was due to be discharged from active service in May 1955, at which time he had planned to finally complete the process of applying to the Foreign Service. But when he confided his plans to Kelsen, the professor offered a characteristically blunt reply. "You are a fool," he told Lowenstein. "You like the law. You have an aptitude for it. Why don't you take a year and go to law school before you submit yourself to the government. You have already wasted three years in the Navy. What difference does a year make?" The clock, however, was ticking. Lowenstein was approaching his 28th birthday and had to be wary of the age limit for entering officers, which was 30. Nevertheless, he decided to embark on what he later called his "law school experiment."[81]

Law school admissions were often informal in the 1950s. One afternoon in fall 1954, Lowenstein strolled into the Yale Law School admissions office to express his interest, only to be told that his undergraduate grades were not strong enough. Harvard Law School, however, was more encouraging: Take the Law School Admission Test (LSAT), they told him, and if he scored in the 90th percentile or above, they would admit him. He took the test, scored in the 90s, was accepted, and enrolled for the following fall.[82]

In the meantime, Lowenstein married. During his time in Newport, he had spent weekends at his parents' home in Greenwich, Connecticut, and it was there he met Dora Richardson. Born in Greensboro, North Carolina, and raised in Greensboro and Greenwich, Dora came from a family of some renown. In 1905, her grandfather, Lunsford Richardson, had founded the Vick Chemical Company, whose most famous product, Vick's VapoRub, a salve for colds, was a household name. Her Southern upbringing was a world away from Lowenstein's in Westchester County and Connecticut. Their wedding was held in June 1955 at the Round Hill Church in Greenwich. After honeymooning in France, the couple settled in Cambridge, Massachusetts, and Lowenstein started classes at Harvard in September.[83]

Lowenstein's first few months at law school went well. Then, two days before the Christmas break, he fell ill. As his symptoms worsened, he visited the campus infirmary, where he was diagnosed with the flu and advised to return home for Christmas. He and Dora drove to New York City to spend the holiday with his parents. But by the time they arrived, he had become lethargic, bordering on comatose. He was rushed by ambulance to Lenox Hill Hospital, and there doctors identified the true cause of the illness: bulbar polio.[84]

The early 1950s had seen a renewed polio outbreak, leaving thousands dead and many more paralyzed, mostly children. It was only when mass vaccinations of the Jonas Salk vaccine began in 1955 that polio was brought under control. The version of polio that Lowenstein contracted attacked the cranial nerves and the muscles they controlled, including those of the head, neck, and diaphragm. It also caused extreme fever. On Christmas Eve, doctors warned Dora and his parents that unless Lowenstein's fever broke within a few hours, he would not survive.

Fortunately, Lowenstein's fever broke and he recovered. The disease had paralyzed part of his face, forever changing his facial expression; otherwise, he was lucky. The only other damage was to the left sternocleidomastoid muscle in his neck, but because this same muscle had been damaged at birth, he had already compensated for the resulting deficiency. After a couple of weeks in the hospital, Lowenstein and Dora went to stay at Dora's family's house in Greensboro, where Lowenstein attended a rehabilitation clinic to recover his voice, strength, and mobility.[85]

By March 1956, when Lowenstein was finally fit enough to return to law school, he had fallen far behind. Two professors, Austin Scott and A. James Casner, blithely told him to drop out. Another professor had a different view. Abrams Chayes, 34, was in his first year teaching at Harvard Law School, the beginning of a brilliant, 40-year career there. He would go on to serve as a legal advisor to the US State Department, in which capacity he had a profound influence over many Cold War foreign policy issues, including the American response to the raising of the Berlin Wall and President John F. Kennedy's handling of the Cuban Missile Crisis. It was Chayes who persuaded Kennedy to frame his response to the Soviet incursion as a quarantine rather than a blockade. Under international law, a blockade could have been deemed an act of war. Perhaps because Lowenstein and Chayes were so close in age, Chayes was far more sympathetic to Lowenstein's situation. "Don't pay any attention to those guys," Chayes said. "You come out to my house on Saturday afternoons, and I'll get you through the first year."

Lowenstein did get through, but just barely. At the end of the academic year, he ranked 360 in a class of 489. He weighed his options. The Law School's dean of students advised: "The world has enough lawyers. You're not interested in the kind of law that your father practices. You're only interested in the international aspect of the law." Had he done well, Lowenstein might have stayed on to finish law school, knowing that a lawyer has more control over his life than a diplomat. Instead he decided to withdraw and throw his lot in with the Foreign Service.[86]

A Foreign Service Officer

It was now summer 1956. Because too much time had passed since he had last taken the Foreign Service written examination, Lowenstein had to sit for the written exam again as well as the oral. He passed both and was assigned to join the Foreign Service class entering in November. In the interim he returned briefly to active duty in the Navy as a full lieutenant, having received a promotion while in the reserves. He spent two months in the office of the Navy Judge Advocate General at the Pentagon, working on a law of the sea project.[87] Finally, in November 1956, he embarked in earnest on the career he had long planned for himself.

That career began when he enrolled in the A-100 course, a six-week orientation for new Foreign Service officers. The class was basic training for diplomats, with lectures on the operation and security of US embassies and consulates and briefings on Capitol Hill and at the Pentagon. Enrollees were asked to give presentations to the class on their previous experience and future interests in the Foreign Service. Some attended language training in the evenings.[88]

Although the State Department had begun to weed out the old guard of the old Foreign Service in favor of a more professional and diverse corps of diplomats, change came slowly. Lowenstein's entering class was made up of students who still came from upper class backgrounds and were educated at Ivy League universities and other elite colleges, although they were varied in age and experience. They were also predominantly male and white.[89] Over time, the State Department would come to see both value and virtue in a Foreign Service that was broadly representative of the American people. When Frances E. Willis was appointed ambassador to Switzerland in 1953, she became the first female Foreign Service officer to head a US embassy.

Lowenstein was entering the Foreign Service at an exciting moment for American diplomacy. The State Department still held considerable influence in the formulation and execution of foreign policy. This was one reason why Michael Sterner, a member of Lowenstein's entering class, chose the Foreign Service over the Central Intelligence Agency, Capitol Hill, and various international organizations. "If I'm going to [be engaged in international affairs]," he said, "I want to be in the organization that provides the greatest opportunity for responsibility and influence in the senior ranks."[90] He eventually became a leading Arabist in the State Department and US ambassador to the United Arab Emirates.

The United States was at the height of its postwar power. The US demonstrated this power during the 1956 Suez Canal crisis. By threatening economic sanctions against Britain and France if they did not abandon their military campaign against Egypt's Gamal Abdel Nasser, the United States hastened the end of European imperialism. Another crisis demonstrated the rising Soviet power: the Hungarian Revolution in the fall of 1956, when Hungarians revolted against Soviet control and the Soviets responded with a military crackdown. This confrontation made clear the Soviet Union's control over the states in Eastern Europe. These two key issues in US foreign policy, the Europe's declining imperialism and the Soviet's increasing control over Eastern states, would figure prominently in Lowenstein's first decade in the Foreign Service.

Office of European Regional Affairs

Members of the A-100 class could bid on their first assignments. Before Lowenstein bid on his, he sought the advice of Benson Ellison Lane Timmons, an American acquaintance from his Marshall Plan days who now headed the State Department's Office of European Regional Affairs (RA) in Washington. Timmons responded with "You're going to come and work for me as my staff assistant."[91]

RA was an influential office in the State Department. As a division of the Bureau of European Affairs (EUR), its job was to support the US relationship with NATO, the Organization for European Economic Cooperation, and other supranational entities of the newly developing European community. This made it the natural bridge between political and economic policymaking on Europe.

Timmons was a formidable leader. He was a Rhodes Scholar and a colonel in the US Army during the war and he served as a military government officer in Italy before joining the Foreign Service, where he became a special assistant to David K. E. Bruce in 1948, when Bruce was head of the Economic Cooperation Administration (ECA) mission to France. Eventually he rose to become director of the Paris office of the Mutual Security Administration, successor to the ECA.[92]

Timmons, then aged 41, was as also demanding—a "brute of a guy" according to Lowenstein. "He would come crashing in about 7 a.m. and tear through all the [overnight] cables…that I had stacked up." Often he would go down to the communications room and hover over the clerks as they decoded even more cables.[93] "He would write furious instructions on about 25 or 30 of these cables," Lowenstein said, "which I would have to pass along. He would issue all sorts of unrealistic orders. Then he would go off to his early morning staff meeting." He kept up this feverish pace all day and well into the evening. This translated into 12-hour days for Lowenstein, who was forced to drop out of his evening legal studies at George Washington University and abandon once and for all any thought of finishing law school.

After Lowenstein had been with Timmons for 18 months, Timmons finally decided to take a vacation. Lowenstein packed up several briefcases full of reports for him to read while he was away, and when he left, there was a collective sigh of relief. Ten days later, promptly at seven o'clock in the morning, Timmons came stomping down the hall like a troop of horses. He entered the office and threw down his bags. "Well, how was the vacation?" Lowenstein asked. "A waste of time like all vacations," Timmons replied, to which his deputy Robert McBride commented, "Well, how would he know? He's never taken one before."[94]

Although Timmons was a difficult boss, his drive and talent were admirable, and Lowenstein became quite fond of him. He saw Timmons as a brilliant bureaucratic maneuverer who exploited RA's position as a clearinghouse for European issues and built a small empire within EUR. One favorite technique of his was to make sure telegrams were not cleared until 5 p.m. By that time most of the other sections of EUR had closed up shop for the night and you could say, "I tried to clear it, but everybody has gone home." Using this tactic to bypass the normal chain of command and control the flow of information, Timmons helped enlarge RA's influence over matters related to Europe.

Lowenstein's time at RA gave him an inside look at some of the most critical issues facing Europe during the Cold War. One was the implications for NATO of German reunification. After West Germany had rearmed and joined NATO in 1955, NATO ministers began to look ahead to the possibility of a unified Germany as part of NATO. This met with bitter resistance from the Soviets, and in early 1957 NATO appointed a Four Power Working Group on German Reunification, composed of representatives from France, Great Britain, the United States, and West Germany. Lowenstein, the staff secretary to the working group, helped draft their report, which included a discussion of Soviet and Allied objectives, potential security measures, and the future status of Germany and Berlin. The prospects for a negotiated settlement with the Soviets over the role of Germany in any collective security arrangement had already been remote when, in November 1958, the Soviets demanded that Western powers withdraw from West Berlin within six months. This sparked a three-year standoff, during which time many negotiations were attempted over the future of West Berlin. It ended in 1961 with the Soviet construction of the Berlin Wall.

Meanwhile, the American security umbrella and a booming economy had given Europeans the luxury to contemplate still closer integration. On March 25, 1957, the six members of the European Coal and Steel Community signed the Treaty of Rome, establishing the European Economic Community (EEC), also known as the Common Market. The treaty provided for the gradual elimination of trade barriers within the member states along with common policies on transportation, agriculture, and relations with nations outside the member states. A companion treaty that established Euratom provided for the coordinated development of civilian nuclear power.

The formation of the EEC marked a significant step on the road to European integration, which raised a fundamental question for policymakers in RA: Did the United States really want a united Europe, which would become an economic competitor to the United States? "The official line was that we wanted it," Lowenstein said, "but we wanted it as long as we could control it and as long as we had the British on our side."[95] The United States ultimately supported European unity, as a united Europe contributed to winning the Cold War. But RA pursued this policy with a light touch, allowing Europeans to move at their own pace toward deeper integration.[96]

US policy on NATO and European integration was presented with a new challenge when Charles de Gaulle returned to power. The leader of Free French forces during the war, he came out of retirement in 1958 to draft a new constitution for France, and he was elected president later that year. De Gaulle's vision of a strong, independent France armed with nuclear weapons clashed with the vision held by the United States and Britain, who had dominant roles in NATO. De Gaulle felt they had marginalized France. In September 1958, he proposed a tripartite "inner" directorate that would put France on an equal footing with the US and Britain by committing the three to make joint political and military decisions.

Timmons was apoplectic, certain that de Gaulle was allowing his own vanity to weaken the Western alliance. Secretary of State John Foster Dulles and most of the rest of the US foreign policy establishment agreed. In their view, giving Britain and France an effective veto over American policy toward NATO risked splitting the alliance.[97] President Eisenhower attempted to reach some accommodation with de Gaulle short of the full tripartite structure that he demanded, but such overtures came to nothing. Christian Herter, Dulles's successor as Secretary of State, blamed this failure on de Gaulle. "It always come down to de Gaulle never agreeing with anyone else but wanting everybody to agree with him."[98]

Lowenstein took a different view. He regarded the American response to de Gaulle as an emotional overreaction, part of a mindset in the State Department that he saw as "viscerally anti-French." Few, he believed, had sufficient appreciation for what de Gaulle had achieved, not only during the war but as a stabilizing force in French politics. Nor did many in the State Department understand how America's own actions served to alienate the French. It was perhaps no coincidence that de Gaulle made his gambit for more influence in NATO just two months after the United States landed Marines in Beirut, Lebanon, to shore up the pro-Western Maronite Christian government without bothering to tell the French, who had historic ties to Lebanon. It was hardly unreasonable, Lowenstein argued, for de Gaulle to demand now a greater voice in the Western alliance.[99]

Ceylon

Lowenstein was told that his next assignment was to be vice consul in Lyon, for which his duties in RA had made him well suited. Three days later, the assignment was abruptly changed, as it often was in the Foreign Service, and he was posted instead to Colombo, Ceylon (today called Sri Lanka), where he was to be the junior political officer.[100] Lowenstein would have been hard-pressed to pinpoint the island country of Ceylon on a map, much less articulate any authoritative knowledge of its relationship to the United States.

Lowenstein bought all the books he could find on Ceylon and packed them away to read on the journey there. He had plenty of time, as he and Dora decided to go by ship, which took several weeks. Their family then included an 18-month-old daughter, Laurinda, and a second child on the way. They packed up a vast store of goods and every conceivable electrical appliance, and sent their belongings ahead for delivery.[101] Then they sailed from New York to Naples and then via the Mediterranean and the Suez Canal to Colombo, where they arrived in December 1958.

A former British colony, Ceylon had gained independence in 1948. For years afterwards, US policy toward Ceylon was one of benign neglect. Then, in 1956, S. W. R. D. Bandaranaike became prime minister, and he quickly joined the Non-Aligned Movement, which was founded that year by Tito of Yugoslavia, its self-proclaimed head. Other members included Nasser of

Egypt, Nehru of India, Sukarno of Indonesia, and Nkrumah of Ghana. They all stuck firmly to a middle path between Communism and Capitalism. This approach gave Bandaranaike influence on the world stage far out of proportion to Ceylon's modest wealth and status.

The United States thereafter promoted much the same policy in Ceylon as it did in Yugoslavia, encouraging Ceylon to resist overtures from the Soviets and remain in the Non-Aligned camp. The US funded a public affairs program involving press and academic exchanges and a small aid program, which Jack Kubisch, Lowenstein's old boss at OSR in Paris, helped administer, that claimed some major accomplishments. The aid funded school nutrition programs, modernized Ceylon's railways by replacing coal-burning engines with diesel-powered coaches, and launched a medical program that controlled and eventually eradicated malaria.[102] And it managed to do so in spite of nominal restrictions on assistance to countries that, like Ceylon, had nationalized assets or had done business with the Soviet Union or China.

Ceylon was Lowenstein's first overseas posting as a career Foreign Service officer, offering him a chance to get into the meat of the work of the Foreign Service. By custom, the junior political officer was assigned to cover internal politics, and in this Lowenstein had the support of the new ambassador, Bernard Gufler, a 30-year veteran of the Foreign Service. The deputy chief of mission in Colombo in the early 1950s, Gufler knew Ceylon well and knew everyone there. With Gufler's encouragement and with access to Gufler's vast Rolodex, Lowenstein got to know everyone in Ceylonese political circles, from the Governor-General and opposition party leaders to journalists and other diplomats. He also traveled up and down the island interviewing mayors and other local officials, falling in love with Ceylon's sublime natural beauty and ideal climate, a mix of temperate and tropical.

The tranquil climate was just one of Ceylon's many advantages. Ceylon had won independence without bloodshed. The school system and civil service, both patterned after the British systems, were of a high standard. It was rich in natural resources, with tea, coconut, and rubber plantations. No other country threatened Ceylon. Ceylonese politicians carried on the British tradition of spirited debate in parliament and easy socializing outside of it. Most of the politicians had been educated at elite British universities: Bandaranaike at Oxford; Dudley Senanayake, head of the centrist UNP party, at Cambridge; Peter Keuneman, leader of the Communist Party, at Cambridge; and Dr. N. M. Perera, head of the Trotskyite LSSP party, at the London School of Economics. Lowenstein saw Ceylon as a country with everything going for it.[103]

And yet the ethnic discord in Ceylon created risks for the country's leadership. Then, as now, the main political issue in Ceylon was the relationship between the island's two main ethnic groups, the majority Buddhist Sinhalese and the minority Hindu Tamils. In recent years, growing political and economic discontent had pitted the two against each other. Bandaranaike and his Sri Lanka Freedom Party (SLFP) had come to power on a platform of Sinhalese nationalism. Their platform included making Sinhalese the sole official language, increasing state support for Buddhism, and implementing economic policies that favored the Sinhalese at the expense of the Tamils, who had long been overrepresented in British colonial institutions. He had also mobilized the Buddhist clergy to support him, which would prove to be his downfall. A 1957 regional autonomy pact negotiated between Bandaranaike and the Tamil leader promptly fell apart, leading to riots the following year in which many Tamils perished. Two of Lowenstein's closest Tamil friends would end up leaving the country out of fear for their safety.

That was the backdrop to the events of September 25, 1959, when Lowenstein became one of the last two men to see Bandaranaike alive. Lowenstein had accompanied Ambassador Gufler to the prime minister's residence, Tintagel at Rosmead Place. An hour later, the prime minister escorted Gufler back to their car. Just as the car passed through the gate, Gufler and Lowenstein heard a popping noise, which they assumed was vehicle backfiring. When they returned to the embassy 20 minutes later, the phone rang in Lowenstein's office. It was Peter Sherman, an officer with MI6 at the British High Commission. "Chap's been shot," Sherman told him. "What chap?" Lowenstein asked. "The prime minister, old boy."[104] Bandaranaike died of his wounds the following day.

The assassin was a disgruntled Buddhist monk named Talduwe Somarama Thero, who had been lying in wait on the porch around the corner from the front entrance of the prime minister's residence. Thero was acting on behalf of extremist elements in the Buddhist clergy who believed Bandaranaike had not been aggressive enough in pursuing his Sinhalese nationalist reforms. When the Ceylonese government appointed a commission to investigate the assassination, Lowenstein was assigned to report on the commission for the US embassy.

It was in the course of this assignment that he developed a friendship with Bradman Weerakoon, the secretary to the commission who would serve nine Ceylonese and Sri Lankan heads of state over a 50-year career. The two would remain close ever after.

A few months later, Bandaranaike's widow managed to form a government, thus becoming the world's first female prime minister. She continued her late husband's policies of Sinhalese nationalism, with protectionist tariffs and other policies that discriminated against Tamils. But she was not the leader her husband was, and her government was short-lived, the first of four different governments over the next two years.

The growing pains of a modern society existed alongside vestiges of colonial life. The house that Lowenstein and his family rented came equipped with a driver, a cook, a houseboy, a housekeeper, a gardener, and someone to handle the snakes that found their way inside—all that any colonial nabob could want. But imperialistic practices cast a shadow. Many private clubs were still segregated by nationality. Lowenstein's second child, his son, Price, was born in a hospital in Colombo called the Joseph Fraser Nursing Home and delivered by a renowned

Tamil woman obstetrician, Dr. Siva Chinnatamby. Dora, as a white woman married to a white man, could give birth there, as could a white woman married to a Ceylonese man. But at that time if the child of the white woman and her Ceylonese husband became sick, the child could not receive care at the hospital.

This lingering segregation presented no issues for Lowenstein and his wife, who mixed freely with Ceylonese and British alike. Dora had many Ceylonese friends, and Lowenstein played tennis at a club whose membership was predominantly Ceylonese. Together, they hosted cocktail parties with Ceylonese politicians and journalists as well as foreign diplomats and businessmen, especially friends from the German, Australian, and Indian missions. They also had close British friends. In addition to the MI6 representative Peter Sherman and his wife, Celia, they developed a lifelong friendship with Lieutenant Commander Peter Troubridge, who ran a British naval wireless station outside of Colombo, and his wife, Venetia. But the British were fast disappearing, as British-owned tea plantations were being nationalized and their owners and workers were leaving. Lowenstein was witnessing the end of a colonial relationship.[105]

Back to Yugoslavia

When George Kennan was appointed US ambassador to Yugoslavia in March 1961, the State Department immediately began casting around for personnel with prior Yugoslav experience, and Lowenstein was tapped. He first would need to complete Serbo-Croatian language training. Lowenstein and his family returned to Washington after spending two and a half years in Ceylon. In August 1961, he began a nine-month training program in the Serbo-Croatian language at the Foreign Service Institute (FSI).

The course was run by two Serbs, Dragutin Popovich and Yanko Yankovich, brothers-in-law who had married sisters. They were from Sabac, a little town about 60 miles outside of

Belgrade on the Sava river. When asked how it was that the State Department's only two Serbo-Croatian speakers came from the same town, they replied that it was in Sabac where the purest Serbo-Croatian was spoken.[106] They had opened a law practice together, which prospered, but when the war came, they became officers in the Royal Serbian Army. They were subsequently captured by the Germans, and they served out the war in a German POW camp. In 1945, they were liberated by American forces, only to lose everything in the Communist takeover. Eventually they found their way to the United States, where they became teachers at FSI.[107]

Popovich and Yankovich were bitterly anti-Communist and anti-Tito. Popovich, by all accounts, was also anti-everyone else. He was an insufferable bigot who reveled in stories about abusing people of other nationalities, mainly Albanians and Jews. One of Lowenstein's FSI classmates recalled that his face lit up as he told the story of Serb mutineers during the First World War being executed by axe. To those who had never been to Yugoslavia, this was a rude introduction to Serbian chauvinism.[108] For Lowenstein it was a reminder of the bitter ethnic tensions that Tito tried to vanquish with his policy of *Bratstvo I Jedinstvo* (Brotherhood and Unity).

The FSI's audio-lingual training method proved highly effective; Lowenstein also had the benefit of his college training in Russian, which used a Cyrillic alphabet. Within a few months, he and his classmates demonstrated proficiency in this complex language. One classmate, John Chapman "Chips" Chester, did exceptionally well on the final oral exam by not only answering questions with technical proficiency, but also turning every answer into a rant against Tito and the Communists. Popovich and Yankovich could not help but appreciate his responses.[109]

Lowenstein joined the Belgrade embassy in the summer of 1962—a rocky period for US-Yugoslav relations. By then, the United States had abandoned any hope of Tito throwing his lot in with the Americans.[110] In fact, Tito had formalized his role as leader of the Non-Aligned Movement at a conference in Belgrade in September 1961. It was thus all the more jarring when at that same conference Tito, who had previously criticized the United States for conducting nuclear tests, failed to condemn the Soviets for their resumption of nuclear testing after a three-year moratorium. Everyone in the US foreign policy establishment was outraged. Congress suspended Yugoslavia's Most-Favored Nation trading status with the United States in retaliation, but soon restored it. Yugoslavia and Poland were unique among Eastern bloc countries in enjoying such status. Tito's betrayal cast a shadow over relations between the US and Yugoslavia during Lowenstein's time in Belgrade, when divining Tito's intentions became a primary goal of US embassy staff.[111]

The Belgrade political section that Lowenstein joined included Richard G. Johnson, the deputy head of the section who would go on to serve as the number two at US embassies in Sofia and Stockholm, and David Anderson, the first US ambassador in Belgrade after Tito's death in 1980. As a recent arrival, Lowenstein started out with responsibility for supervising the preparation of the daily press summary. These synopses of Yugoslav media coverage of the daily affairs and political issues, translated into English by Yugoslav employees of the embassy, equipped US embassy staff to deal with Yugoslav officials throughout the country.[112]

The press summary was a common practice in US embassies at the time, and it played an important role in Yugoslavia, where neither a free press nor foreign newspapers existed, although Yugoslavs with shortwave radios could use those to access Western news sources, such as the British Broadcasting Corporation and Voice of America. Political officers looked to the press summary as a source of insight into internal Communist party debates—who was up and who was down, what was happening in the political establishments at the republic level, the significance of laws passed by the Federal Assembly, and signs of ethnic tension. "The Communist press was one way that Communists communicated with each other," recalled Harry Dunlop, one of Lowenstein's colleagues in the political section. The press summary provided a window into "what the Yugoslav Government wanted the world to learn about what they thought" concerning a particular policy or event.[113]

In his first months in Belgrade, Lowenstein also worked closely with the author of a new Yugoslav constitution, employing the normative analytical techniques he had learned from Hans Kelsen during his stint at the Naval War College. That constitution, Yugoslavia's third since it was founded in 1945, came into effect on April 7, 1963. It established a new federal assembly with one general chamber and four smaller bodies that functioned as the equivalent of workers' councils. Tito was nominally subordinate to the federal assembly, although his Communist party retained control by means of elections to the assembly. This tension was the focus of an article Lowenstein later published called "Yugoslavia: Parliamentary Model?" The article appeared in the respected United States Information Agency journal *Problems of Communism*:

> What is the significance of the new Yugoslav Assembly? Those who view it in a favorable light see it as an evolutionary step towards further democratization, paving the way for the expression of more liberal political tendencies in Yugoslav society, providing a forum for more discussion and debate on national policies, and giving Yugoslav citizens a greater voice in the selection of their representatives. To others more critical, the new Assembly appears to represent primarily an attempt to legitimize the regime, to give the Yugoslav people the illusion but not the reality of free elections, and to perpetuate party control in a more subtle and palatable fashion. Like so much else in a country noted for contrasts and contradictions, the new Assembly may be all of these things.[114]

Lowenstein was assigned to focus on internal political affairs, which he preferred to external political affairs. "The external involved running down to the foreign office and exchanging notes and reporting views. You didn't learn what's going on in the country because that wasn't your job. You didn't have any real insight into the country as a basis for any kind of original analysis. I always preferred internal reporting."[115]

Like any good reporter, Lowenstein worked his sources. He talked to diplomats in other Western embassies who had good connections throughout Yugoslavia. These included an officer in the Norwegian embassy, Thorvald Stoltenberg, who would go on to become a defense minister and foreign minister as well as a lifelong friend. Stoltenberg's son, Jens, is now Secretary-General of NATO. He cultivated friendships with David Binder of the *New York Times* and Anatole Shub of the *Washington Post*, both leading correspondents covering Central and Eastern Europe. He also talked to the few Yugoslavs in Belgrade who would talk to him. Often, political officers like Lowenstein learned much of what they knew from local Yugoslav employees of the embassy, although their views were predominately anti-Communist because they usually came from upper middle class families that had lost prospects or fortunes in the Communist takeover.[116]

Lowenstein supplemented what he learned from the press and personal contacts by participating in an embassy program of travel around the country.[117] Every six months or so, members of the political section paired up with their opposite numbers in the economic section for 10-day field-reporting trips.[118] Lowenstein was paired with a friend from his Serbo-Croatian language class, Lawrence Eagleburger, a particularly gifted career Foreign Service officer who would go on to run the embassy in Belgrade and later serve as US deputy and acting Secretary of State. The two were sometimes joined by Thomas M. T. Niles, a newly-minted Foreign Service officer who would go on to become ambassador to Canada, Greece, and the European Union.

Traveling by jeep along Yugoslavia's back roads, the trio visited local authorities at the *Opstina* (village council) level, which usually included the mayor and his deputy. No matter the time of day, they were offered a ritual glass of slivovitz, a plum brandy beloved throughout Eastern Europe. Eagleburger and Niles both accepted; Lowenstein declined, as he drank only wine. "By one o'clock in the afternoon, the driving naturally fell to me, with [the other two] conked out in the back seat," he said. They also called on youth organizations and labor unions, and interacted with people in cafes and restaurants and at open-air markets, which brought in farmers from miles around.[119] Along the way, they took in Yugoslavia's spectacular mix of coastal and mountain scenery. One particularly beautiful route took them from Belgrade down through Sarajevo and Mostar, along the Dalmatian coast, and back up through Montenegro.

Although they were free to travel wherever they liked, Lowenstein and other embassy officials could not expect anyone in a position of authority to talk with them unless they had cleared their itineraries in advance with the Foreign Ministry. Even then, permission was not always communicated to local officials. That was the case for one team led by Richard Johnson. They found themselves escorted out of town by the Služba Državne Bezbednosti (the Yugoslav secret police), who kept track of US embassy personnel and their movements. Traveling in pairs or groups also made it less likely that government officials could stage a provocation or put an embassy officer in a compromising position.[120]

Such obstacles aside, the field-reporting trips gave Lowenstein a good sense of a country that, despite considerable liberalization relative to other Communist regimes, had not embraced meaningful reforms of its Marxist-Leninist economic system. He did not, however, find Yugoslavs chafing under a regime that had deprived them of their democratic rights. Rather, he observed, the establishment of workers' councils had provided them with participation in the formulating government policies that affected their lives and an appreciation for how their lives were better than those of people in other Communist countries. Also, people were allowed to travel, the shops and restaurants were full, and intellectuals and journalists mixed more or less freely with their western counterparts.[121]

In addition to traveling throughout Yugoslavia, Lowenstein took advantage of his time in Belgrade to visit other countries in the Balkans and Eastern Europe. He and Dora spent several long weekends in Sofia, Bulgaria, as guests of his former Belgrade embassy colleague, Richard Johnson, and his wife, Pat. He visited Bucharest, Romania, with Emil Guikovati, head of the Agence France Presse office in Belgrade, who was going there to interview Nicolae Ceaușescu, then the number two figure in the Romanian Communist party. He spent a week in Warsaw, Poland, with Anatole Shub, the *Washington Post*'s Eastern European correspondent. And he made several weekend trips to Budapest, Hungary, a three-hour drive from Belgrade. These exposures to other countries in the region gave him a valuable perspective on how different was the path that Tito had chosen for Yugoslavia.

Yet although Yugoslavia projected the illusion of a country that had moved beyond the bitter nationalisms of its past, it had not. Tito kept a firm hold on ethnic discord. He maintained a policy of rotating military and party leaders outside of their own republics. When there was an outbreak of ethnic violence, he would simply replace the person in charge. It was therefore reasonable for Lowenstein to predict that Yugoslavia's high inter-marriage rates would eliminate ethnic distinctions within a generation or two. He was mistaken. "The Yugoslavia we served in did not permit nationalist excesses," recalled Thomas Niles, "but it was there, under the surface. The younger people with whom I associated, people in their twenties, sang those [nationalist] songs, but they were careful. Serbian nationalism was under wraps."[122] Of course, it was not long after Tito's death in 1980 that those jealousies and resentments burst into the open, with catastrophic results.

Lowenstein had been told by someone who had known Ambassador Kennan well that he might find Kennan a bit distant, which turned out to be true. He actually saw very little of Kennan, who cut an elegant figure in US diplomatic circles and was generally too busy to take much notice of Lowenstein or other embassy junior staff. The one exception was Lowenstein's friend, R. Gerald Livingston. A member of the economic section with a PhD from Harvard, Livingston had done research in Belgrade and Zagreb as a graduate student and spoke fluent Serbo-Croatian. "I wouldn't say he took a shine to me," Livingston recalled, "but he had this project of getting officers to write up little studies…and I enjoyed it. I wrote a study of 19th century Serbia, a couple of Obrenović kings or something, and Kennan liked that."[123]

Kennan was also rather stiff in his manner and highly sensitive to perceived slights. He felt personally insulted when Tito failed to condemn the Soviets for announcing they would resume nuclear tests; Lowenstein found Kennan to be still fuming that about when he arrived in Belgrade a year after the Soviet announcement.[124]

Kennan's successor, who arrived in January 1964, could not have been more different from Kennan. C. Burke Elbrick had been Assistant Secretary of State for European Affairs, and Lane Timmons' boss when Lowenstein was a staff aide to Timmons. A former ambassador to Portugal, he would later go on to head the embassy in Brazil. Lowenstein saw Elbrick as "approachable, open, funny, very experienced, and seemingly effortless in everything he did." He was also far more sociable, and he included Lowenstein and his fellow junior embassy officers in the dinners he hosted for Yugoslav officials and American official visitors at his residence.

Though Lowenstein's posting to Belgrade had put him closer to the heart of US foreign policy, he did not enjoy his time there quite as much as his time in Colombo, Ceylon. He thought his family's first housing assignment, an apartment in the embassy compound, was a nightmare, as he was accustomed to socializing with local people and expatriates. His children, however, adored it as they were able to play with other children in the inner courtyard. After a year, he was moved to a small, prefabricated house on the grounds of the ambassador's residence, which improved his situation. So did the arrival of Adolph "Spike" Dubs as the new head of the embassy's political section. Dubs eventually became the US ambassador to Afghanistan and was kidnapped in 1979 and killed in a failed rescue attempt.

In October 1964, in the middle of his third year in Belgrade, Lowenstein's daughter, Laurinda, then aged six, suffered a concussion and broken teeth when their Norwegian babysitter accidentally drove the family's Volkswagen into a parked car. The embassy's medical facilities were minimal, and despite days of trying, Lowenstein could not get permission to evacuate her. Eventually his mother-in-law arranged to fly in her doctor, who took the girl back to the United States for treatment. Lowenstein left soon after, six months before his tour was scheduled to end.

Lowenstein was now back in Washington working on US policy related to the new United Nations Conference on Trade and Development (UNCTAD). Compared to his postings at the Colombo and Belgrade embassies, he found the ins-and-outs of the UN bureaucracy less stimulating. What kept up his spirits was an invitation from Joseph Greenwald, the deputy assistant secretary and a future ambassador to the European Union, to join him for the next round of OECD meetings in Paris. Greenwald offered an appealing enticement, saying, "If I put you on the delegation with me, can we play tennis?"

Lowenstein had another lucky break when a friend from the past came back into his life. While he had been in Ceylon, he had volunteered to host a Congressional visit by Senator Bourke B. Hickenlooper of Iowa, then the ranking Republican member of the Senate Foreign Relations Committee. Accompanying him was a Committee staffer and former print and broadcast journalist, John Newhouse. When a monsoon hit, Hickenlooper and Newhouse were grounded, and Lowenstein and Dora put up Newhouse for the night. The two men became friends, bonding over shared memories of the time each had spent in Paris in their youth. A few years later, while he was in Yugoslavia, Lowenstein volunteered to escort another American visitor: Carl Marcy, the Committee's chief of staff, who had stopped in Belgrade during a study mission to the Balkans, and they and their wives toured the Yugoslav countryside. "Everybody else thought it was pain in the neck" to shepherd Congressional officials around, Lowenstein recalled; "I thought it was fascinating to meet these people."[125]

Fascinating, and, as it turned out, useful to his career. Lowenstein had been back in Washington for only a few weeks when he received a call from Marcy. "Your old friend John Newhouse has just left the Senate Foreign Relations Committee staff, and Fulbright thinks he would like a Foreign Service officer to enter the competition to replace him." Lowenstein welcomed the chance. From an initial list of six or seven other candidates, three finalists, including Lowenstein, were chosen by a subcommittee of two ranking majority and two ranking minority members of the Committee. He then interviewed with Senator William Fulbright of Arkansas and Senator George Aiken of Vermont, by then the ranking Republican on the Committee. He got the job.[126]

Going to work on Capitol Hill meant leaving the Foreign Service with no guarantee of return, though Marcy, who had helped draft the Foreign Service Act that governed ties with the legislative branch, waved away such concerns. "You can take a leave and then go back," he assured Lowenstein. But that was the last thing Lowenstein's mind just then. "My only concern on going up to the Committee was that…I might be trading one job that I didn't think was very interesting for another one that I didn't think would be very interesting." In fact, he was about to embark on the most compelling chapter in his career.

3 Capitol Hill

Fulbright and the Senate Foreign Relations Committee

Lowenstein's first day on Capitol Hill set the tone for his next nine years there. He arrived in his new office at the Committee to begin his work with the small bi-partisan staff. He had barely settled in when the telephone rang. One of Senator Fulbright's secretaries said: "Senator Fulbright wondered whether you might be free to have lunch with him today." As Lowenstein describes that lunch:

> A few hours later the Senator and I entered the Senate dining room. Senator Russell, the Chairman of the Senate Armed Services Committee was sitting alone at a table. Senator Fulbright asked him to join us. I thought to myself that here I was, after just a few hours, sitting with two of the most powerful members of the Senate.
>
> Just then the waitress arrived. The two senators greeted her by name. She reciprocated and then said: "What are you two boys having today?" Senator Russell said that he would like the cottage cheese salad but

with a peach instead of a pear (canned, needless to say). Senator Fulbright said he would have the same. The waitress put her hands on her hips and said: "Now you boys know there are no substitutions." Both apologized, and the salad was served with canned pears. I thought that this incident proved that if two powerful senators could not have a canned peach instead of a canned pear, democracy was alive and well.

And on the subject of democracy, after lunch I accompanied Senator Fulbright to his office. As I was leaving, he asked me when I had last read de Tocqueville. I replied that it had been some time. He took the two volumes, shoved them across the desk and said that I had better read them again. I mentioned it to Carl Marcy, the Committee Chief of Staff. He said that, in his speeches, Fulbright quoted de Tocqueville more than any other single source.

The deference to the egalitarian rules of the Senate dining room was not the only characteristic that defined the Senate of the 1960s. Despite fierce struggles over civil rights legislation, an atmosphere of political comity and mutual respect prevailed. It was also a time of broad, bipartisan consensus on foreign policy, forged in response to the perceived threat of Communism.

The custodian of this consensus was the Senate Foreign Relations Committee. One of the Senate's 10 original standing committees, the Committee reviewed treaties and related legislation. It also had jurisdiction over diplomatic appointments and oversight responsibilities for the State Department. The 19 members of the Committee were intelligent and had good political instincts. "Just remember two things about senators," Carl Marcy joked to Lowenstein. "First, when the vast majority of them look in the mirror in the morning, they see a future president of the United States. Second, it is very difficult to be elected a senator if you're stupid."[127] Marcy might have been thinking of W. Stuart

Symington of Missouri, a senator with finely-tuned political instincts and obvious presidential ambitions. Symington was a vocal critic of McCarthyism and a two-time candidate for the Democratic Presidential nomination. He responded to the June 1972 break-in of the Democratic National Committee headquarters with suspicion, even as newspapers were reporting it as a run-of-the-mill burglary. "Hmmm, there's more here than meets the eye," he said to Lowenstein when they met the morning after the story broke.[128] It eventually became the first act in the Watergate scandal.

Members of the Senate Foreign Relations Committee understood the limits of their role, which was not to make American foreign policy but to support it or seek to change it. They behaved with a sense of decorum, even camaraderie. They "thought of themselves as a totality," said Marcy. Far from remaining stuck in ideologically-driven positions, most senators on the Committee respected the facts. "There was a very freewheeling exchange between them," Marcy said. "Minds were changed. Very few members enunciated an idea, and stuck with it…."[129]

This atmosphere owed everything to Fulbright, a complex figure. Although he had been a staunch opponent of civil rights in the past—he had signed the segregationist Southern Manifesto, filibustered the Civil Rights Act of 1964, opposed the 1965 Voting Rights Act, and opposed the 1968 Fair Housing Act—there was a more progressive side to Fulbright. A Rhodes Scholar at Oxford in the late 1920s, he became a classic liberal internationalist who saw multilateral institutions as crucial to world peace and prosperity. He would go on to create the landmark academic and cultural exchange program that bears his name. His steadfast opposition to the war in Vietnam gave him enormous sway over American foreign policy during the 1960s and 1970s. The press often referred to him as the "powerful chairman of the Senate Foreign Relations Committee," with the implication that he imposed his will on his fellow senators. But he actually behaved more like a president of a university, which he had been—he was appointed to head the University of Arkansas in 1939 at age 34, making him the youngest head of an American college at the time. Fulbright listened to people and then persuaded them to his way of thinking. When Senator Symington changed his mind about the Vietnam War, he credited Fulbright. "Bill educated me. I've learned," Symington said.[130]

The Committee was supported by a staff of eight consultants. The staff was strictly non-partisan. They were hired "solely on the basis of merit and without regard to political considerations," as provided under the Legislative Reorganization Act of 1946. During his interview for the staff position, Lowenstein was never asked about his political beliefs or party affiliation, just his experience and opinions on various foreign policy issues.[131] Today there are separate staffs, one for the majority party and one for the minority party.

The staff of the Senate Foreign Relations Committee was an unusually talented group—"comparable to the highest-level of an academic department in a first-rate university," according to Senator Clifford Case of New Jersey.[132] A few had PhDs, such as Seth Tillman, a former assistant professor of political science at the Massachusetts Institute of Technology, who drafted most of Fulbright's speeches. But most had extensive experience in journalism or government, including several who had spent a decade or more working on the Committee or for Fulbright himself.[133]

Chief of Staff Carl Marcy had earned a PhD in international law and relations from Columbia University, where he was also a lecturer. He joined the State Department in 1943 as a legal advisor and legislative counsel before moving to the staff of the Senate Foreign Relations Committee in 1950. He became chief of staff in 1955, and was a savvy operator with a gift for media relations. He maintained active contacts throughout the executive branch—he had a direct line to Dean Rusk, Lyndon Johnson's Secretary of State—and encouraged Committee staff to do the same. He saw their responsibilities as analogous to "a private law or consulting firm, available on call for 19 clients with varied interests," although he also urged staffers to establish what he called "lawyer-client" relationships with individual senators, which he believed made his job easier. Such a relationship entailed each staffer acting as an advocate, researcher, and advisor for his senator and keeping all conversations confidential.[134]

By the time Lowenstein arrived in the Senate, staffers had become key players on Capitol Hill. With the increasing scale and complexity of government during the postwar era, even the most experienced legislator now needed to delegate significant duties to professional staff, whose roles expanded accordingly. Lowenstein and other staffers of the Senate Foreign Relations Committee, for example, helped draft legislation, prepared floor statements and public speeches, negotiated with the staffs of other committees and the offices of individual senators, and often contributed to the books and articles that appeared under a senator's name. It was a demanding job. As Symington said: "I don't see how the [staff] on this Committee can stay healthy with the amount of work that they put in…."[135]

No senator on the Committee engaged with its consultants more closely than Fulbright. "There used to be a certain amount of grousing that Fulbright monopolized the staff," Tillman remembered. "[I would say] that he *magnetized* the staff…He just had this appetite for information and ideas. You knew, as a member of the staff, that if you did a memo, Fulbright was going to read it." Lowenstein found Fulbright to be the perfect boss. "He always gave you credit for what you did. He never blamed you for your mistakes…He was just a marvelous man."[136]

Lowenstein was first assigned to cover Europe, beginning with a review of the *Consular Convention Between the Soviet Union and the United States*. It was signed in Moscow in June 1964 and presented to the Senate for approval one year later. It provided protections for citizens of each country in the territory of the other, especially those arrested or imprisoned; it also promoted commercial and cultural relations between the Cold War rivals.[137] For many Democratic senators on the

Committee, this was utterly uncontroversial. Hardline anti-Communists in both parties, however, had more trouble with it. Lowenstein was therefore asked to prepare two reports on the Convention, one for the majority and one for the minority. This required putting himself in the mind of the senator taking a particular position, and then structuring arguments for or against the Convention. Republican Senator Karl E. Mundt of South Dakota, who had opposed ratifying the Convention, complimented Lowenstein for producing a minority report that he regarded as sounder and more cogently argued than the majority report.[138]

What most senators on the Committee had in common, regardless of party, was a visceral dislike of the French and French president Charles de Gaulle in particular. De Gaulle's assertions of independence seemed calculated to rankle American policymakers, who saw Western European unity as a bulwark against the return of old nationalist rivalries. But for Lowenstein, who was well acquainted with France, the anti-French sentiment among senators on the Committee bordered on the absurd. "The French were general whipping boys for everything that was going wrong in the world," he recalled. "De Gaulle…was constantly being criticized." Lowenstein conducted an experiment to confirm his hypothesis. He gathered several of de Gaulle's recent speeches on Europe and Indochina, struck de Gaulle's name from the attributions, and presented the speeches to Fulbright as the work of a like-minded thinker on foreign policy. "These are very interesting and I must say I agree with everything the fellow says. Who is he?" Fulbright asked Lowenstein. "The fellow is Charles de Gaulle, Senator." "You don't say," the senator replied.[139]

Lowenstein believed that neither de Gaulle's foreign policy aims nor any European issue could be understood in isolation, and he urged Fulbright to conduct broader hearings on US foreign policy toward Europe. "It is useless to talk with Arms Control and Disarmament Agency and Department of Defense officials about non-proliferation," he wrote in March 1966, "without talking about Germany's desire to share in nuclear defense, Soviet opposition to this desire, and French attitudes toward Germany and Eastern Europe...."[140] If no hearings were possible, Lowenstein added, then Fulbright should send a senator to visit a few European countries and attend the Conference of the Eighteen Nation Disarmament Committee in Geneva. Almost immediately, Fulbright asked Senator Frank Church, Democrat of Idaho, to go to Europe and take Lowenstein with him, with the idea that such a trip would form the basis of hearings. The visit, Fulbright assured Church, would signal to the Johnson administration that the Committee was interested in these European issues and determined to examine them seriously.[141]

Lowenstein accompanied Church to Europe in May 1966. The senator's work pace was legendary in the Senate. As one of Church's legislative staffers said: "When Frank Church works, everybody works. And when Frank Church plays, everybody works."[142] After spending three weeks with Church, Lowenstein had nothing but admiration for him. The trip started with a stop in Geneva to allow Church to consult with Jacques Freymond, the Swiss political historian at the Graduate Institute of International Studies. They then went on to meetings with de Gaulle in Paris, Harold Wilson in London, Ludwig Erhard in Bonn, and Joseph Luns, Secretary General of NATO, in Brussels. Church was a lightning-quick study of US foreign policy in Europe. At a dinner following a meeting in Bonn with the US ambassador, George McGhee, the senator gave a brilliant, impromptu overview of US-European relations that dazzled everyone there.[143]

After the Church trip and the hearings that followed, Fulbright and many members of the Senate Foreign Relations Committee changed their attitude toward France. It was too simple to blame de Gaulle for everything that American policymakers believed was going wrong in Europe, Fulbright argued to his fellow Committee members. De Gaulle "may have sharpened the issues, he may have acted precipitately and abruptly, but the questions he has raised have been weighing for some time. We do not answer these questions, or even understand them, by dismissing them out of hand."[144]

In the meantime, Marcy suggested that Lowenstein adapt his report of the Church trip for *Foreign Affairs,* the journal of the Council on Foreign Relations, publishing it under Church's name. The magazine accepted the article on the condition that Lowenstein strike a passage in the final paragraph quoting political columnist Walter Lippman. Lowenstein later discovered why: nearly 30 years earlier, *Foreign Affairs* editor Hamilton Fish Armstrong's wife had divorced him to marry Lippman.[145]

The article contained insights gleaned from the European trip and testimony from the hearings that followed, as well as Lowenstein's own views of US foreign policy toward a changing Europe. It argued that de Gaulle's actions, including his surprise announcement in June 1966 that France would withdraw from integrated military structure of NATO, expressed the desire of European countries to exert control over their own destinies after a long postwar era in America's shadow. The sooner American policymakers recognized this, the better. "It is not the kind of Europe *we* want that any longer governs," the article insisted. "The question is really what kind of resurgent Europe the Europeans themselves will build."[146]

The Church trip was the first of many that Lowenstein made with senators during the late 1960s. One, with Senator Claiborne Pell of Rhode Island, found him in Czechoslovakia shortly before the August 1968 Soviet invasion. Whereas many observers had discounted the possibility of military action in response to mass protests and political liberalization in the Communist state, Lowenstein correctly predicted that the "Prague Spring," by threatening a breakdown in the international Communist order, made Soviet action more likely, not less.[147] Nor, after the fact, did Lowenstein accept the conventional wisdom that the invasion would inevitably strengthen the reformers' hand in Czechoslovakia, and he was not afraid to push back on Pell when he wanted to make a statement on the Senate floor along those lines. "I would personally suggest [a speech that] stated both sides of the argument," he counseled Pell. "Such a speech might redound more to your credit as an Eastern European observer than one which simply repeated the thesis that the seeds of freedom will flourish no matter what and that reactionary governments can't last in the long run."[148]

Lowenstein also made numerous trips to Asia with Mike Mansfield of Montana, the Senate Majority Leader. Quiet and unassuming for a politician of his stature, Mansfield was literally a man of few words. As Lowenstein describes the senator:

> During the summer Senate recess, Senator Mansfield, the Senate Majority Leader, sometimes traveled to Asia. His interest in Asia went back to his time as a Marine in China at the end of World War I. He had also taught Asian history at the Montana State University (now the University of Montana) before becoming a Senator and since then had traveled to Asia often. That experience showed when he met Asians—he was a man of few words and he was perfectly comfortable with long silences. For these summer recess trips, the President gave him an Air Force presidential flight plane. He typically took with him his wife Maureen, an Army doctor, often the Secretary of the Senate, Francis Valeo, and an administrative person, and on two occasions he took me as a general assistant responsible for writing whatever was necessary—the memoranda of conversation, the final report, any statements.
>
> On my first trip with him, the first stop was Tokyo. As we got underway I asked him whether he would like a draft arrival statement. The answer was no. I then asked whether he would like talking points or a statement for his meeting with the Prime Minister. Same response. When we landed in Tokyo, we were met by a large group of journalists, mics and cameras at the ready. The Senator descended from the plane, greeted the

group, said "see you later," and got into the Embassy car waiting for him. Shortly thereafter we met with the Prime Minister, Eisaku Satō. I attended the meeting as note taker. When we emerged, again a large group of the press awaited. The Prime Minister made the usual kind of statement—that it was an honor to receive the Senator, he appreciated the chance to exchange views, the visit had contributed to the understanding between the two countries, etc. He then invited the Senator to the podium. Senator Mansfield turned to the Prime Minister and said: "Thanks and so long." When we got into the car, I said to him that now I understood why he did not want any pro forma statements. He smiled.

In addition to his deep knowledge of Asia and its concerns, Mansfield also boasted personal friendships with many Asian leaders, which often came as a surprise to local embassy officials. As Lowenstein describes a meeting with General Ne Win of Rangoon, Burma, whom the embassy had thought was unapproachable:

One of our other visits was to be to Rangoon. A few days before our arrival, the Senator asked me to send a message to the Ambassador telling him that as soon as he arrived he wanted to see Ne Win, the general who had taken control of the country in a military coup and was running it with an iron hand. Back came a message saying something along the lines of no one sees Ne Win, he doesn't receive foreigners, the Embassy had no contact with him, etc. I showed the reply to the Senator. He made no comment.

Two days later we landed in Rangoon. The Ambassador, Arthur Hummel, was at the foot of the gangway to meet us. He welcomed the Senator and said that we would all be going back to the Embassy for dinner and a briefing and that the next day—at which point the Senator interrupted him and said that he wanted to see Ne Win immediately. Ambassador Hummel asked whether I had not shown Senator Mansfield his reply. The Senator said that I had and that if the Ambassador couldn't take him to see Ne Win, perhaps the Chief of Protocol, who had also met the plane, could. I am sure that Ambassador Hummel thought that the Senator was confused or worse, but he rallied and said that of course if the Senator wanted to see Ne Win, we would go immediately to the presidential palace.

When we arrived, Ne Win came down the stairs to greet us, accompanied by Madame Ne Win, also known as Kitty. She literally jumped into the Senator's arms and said how happy she was to see him. At the same time, Ne Win, calling Mrs. Mansfield by her first name Maureen, had embraced her and welcomed her to Burma. Kitty then announced that dinner had been prepared for the Senator and the group "in the kitchen" and that she was doing the cooking. She turned to Ambassador Hummel and said that of course he was welcome to come to dinner as well. We then all descended to the basement of the palace, where a number of cooks and attendants were busy at work. Kitty supervised them. The dinner was composed of the Senator's favorite fare—overdone roast beef, string beans, and baked potatoes.

After dinner, when we were in the car taking us to the hotel, I said to the Senator that I would be interested in the background to this rather extraordinary evening. The Senator replied in two sentences. Sentence one: "Kitty went to Catholic University in Washington." Sentence two: "When she was there, she often stayed with us."[149]

Leaders like Ne Win of Burma, Prince Norodom Sihanouk of Cambodia, and Ferdinand Marcos of the Philippines trusted Mansfield. He trusted them, too, because they promised stability in a region unsettled by decolonization and ideological conflict. "He felt that they were…authentic, popular political leaders and not artificial creations of either the West or the Communist world," and that only they could hold their countries together and check the spread of Communism.[150]

"Somebody Wasn't Telling the Truth"

The work of the Senate Foreign Relations Committee and its staff was unfolding against the backdrop of a deepening American involvement in Vietnam—the focus of Lowenstein's most important contributions on Capitol Hill. Lyndon Johnson had inherited a deteriorating situation in the region, with South Vietnam struggling to maintain its independence against the Communist North Vietnamese and Viet Cong forces despite millions in US military assistance and hundreds of US military advisers on the ground. At any point Johnson might have abandoned this policy and chosen a different path. Instead, he and his advisers saw no alternative but to make a stand in Indochina, convinced that success there, or at least the absence of failure, was the only way to preserve American credibility and discourage Soviet expansionism.[151] In the process, Johnson became something of a tragic figure, trapped between his domestic and foreign policies. Worried that a Congressional debate over Vietnam would cost him his ambitious Great Society agenda, he was never willing to level with Congress or the American public about the true costs of the war.[152]

The deceit and obfuscation at the heart of Johnson's Vietnam policy was not yet apparent to most on Capitol Hill when Lowenstein arrived there in June 1965. Both houses of Congress had voted Johnson near-unanimous support—first with the Tonkin Gulf resolution in August 1964 and then, after Johnson won election in a landslide, with a $700 million supplemental appropriation in March 1965. Such easy victories no doubt encouraged Johnson to ignore Congress in the fateful decisions he took over the following months, including intensifying air attacks and introducing US combat forces.[153]

Most Congressional Republicans supported Johnson's policy of escalation on the merits; most Democrats did not, but they resisted making an open break with a President of their own party, preferring to express their reservations privately.[154] In a prophetic warning, Mansfield wrote to Johnson that the United States was on a course in Vietnam "which takes us further and further out on a sagging limb." In time, he added, the country could find itself saddled with "enormous burdens in Cambodia, Laos, and elsewhere in Asia, along with those in Vietnam." McGeorge Bundy, Johnson's first National Security Advisor, dismissed such memos from Mansfield as no more than "mousy stubbornness."[155]

Fulbright valued his long-standing close personal relationship with Johnson, who had cleared the way for him to chair the Senate Foreign Relations Committee and later tried to get him appointed as John F. Kennedy's Secretary of State. Fulbright was also the consummate insider, and he believed he could persuade the President against continued escalation. The writer David Halberstam said of Fulbright: "Being an adversary was not a role he had sought under any conditions; it was out of character…[He] liked playing the game."[156]

That changed in April 1965 with the crisis in the Dominican Republic, when soldiers attempted to restore to power the former democratically-elected president, Juan Bosch, who had been overthrown in a coup d'état a year and a half earlier. Johnson was loath to support Bosch, worried that his ties to the country's Communist left would lead the Dominican Republic to become another Cuba. Pointing to accounts of murders and decapitations by the Bosch government, Johnson ordered 400 US Marines ashore to safeguard US and other foreign nationals, with thousands more American troops arriving within hours. When an investigation by Pat Holt, a Latin American specialist on the Senate Foreign Relations Committee staff, revealed Johnson's claims of violence to be exaggerated or false, Fulbright was outraged and made a statement opposing the Dominican intervention on September 15.[157]

It was a mild speech, careful to criticize policies, not personalities, but it sent a chill through the White House, where Johnson and his advisors worried that the address would undermine the fragile support for the war. Indeed, Fulbright's speech would be "the first crack in the Cold War consensus," according to foreign policy analyst Daniel Yergin, and a catalyst for growing Congressional opposition toward America's role in Vietnam.[158]

Fulbright began to take a closer look at the war, which had been less important to him than European matters. Besides reading deeply about the history of Indochina, he sought out anyone with first-hand knowledge of the region.[159] He had Lowenstein track down Bernard Fall, a French-American journalist who had published a widely-acclaimed book on the French war in Indochina, *Street Without Joy* (1961), and invite him to have lunch with the senator. "That was typical Fulbright," Lowenstein recalled. "Find somebody who really knew what he was talking about...and see what he has to say."[160] Fulbright and Fall developed a rapport. When Fall was later killed by a Viet Cong landmine while on patrol with US Marines in February 1967, his widow asked Fulbright to speak at his memorial service. Lowenstein drafted the senator's remarks.[161]

Fulbright also launched a series of high-profile hearings on the American role in Vietnam. For five days in February 1966, retired generals and foreign policy analysts testified in the Senate Caucus Room, weighing in on the implications of American policy in Southeast Asia. Attention peaked with the appearance of Dean Rusk and General Maxwell D. Taylor, Chairman of the Joint Chiefs of Staff, who endured harsh questioning from Fulbright and fellow members of the Senate Foreign Relations Committee. Fulbright was not seeking to make a splash with the hearings, but that is just what he did. The hearings reached some 30 million viewers, giving the nation its first serious public debate over the war and helping to legitimize the growing anti-war movement, even though

CBS suspended its live television broadcast of the hearings at one point in favor of *I Love Lucy* reruns.[162] The hearings, in turn, became the model by which Fulbright sought to influence Vietnam policy: not by legislation (at least not yet), but through relentless public opposition designed to chip away at the consensus in favor of the war.[163]

Meanwhile, Lowenstein's views were evolving. Though he had no strong opinion of the war when he arrived on Capitol Hill, Lowenstein was moved when Senator Philip Hart of Michigan turned against our involvement in Vietnam. Lowenstein witnessed Senator Hart's conversion during a stop they made together in Vietnam in 1967. A lieutenant colonel in the US Army who had been wounded in the D-Day invasion, Hart was no shrinking violet when it came to military commitments. His ardent support for civil rights legislation and his willingness to take on big business, often at the expense of his own political interests, had earned him a reputation as "The Conscience of the Senate." He brought the same moral sensibility with him to Vietnam, where he talked with scores of Michigan troops deployed there. As he and Lowenstein listened to General William Westmoreland, head of US military forces in the region, drone on about enemy body counts, Hart turned to Lowenstein and whispered, "Makes you wonder whose sons they are."[164]

For Lowenstein, the trip to Vietnam offered first-hand evidence of the mendacity of Johnson's Vietnam policy. While Hart was off visiting the troops, Lowenstein tracked down an old friend, the journalist and author Charles Bracelen Flood, who was in the middle of a year as an embedded correspondent with American forces. The two men had known each other since college—Flood at Harvard, Lowenstein at Yale. Lowenstein and Flood were dropped by helicopter into a safe village, where they planned to spend the night. When they awoke the following morning, they discovered that three people in the house of the deputy village chief had been murdered. If this was a safe village, Lowenstein asked himself, what was it like in a contested village? He thought, "It began to look to me as though somebody wasn't telling the truth."[165]

Lowenstein's subsequent trip report made clear his skepticism of official war accounts. "A visitor to Vietnam can find evidence to confirm or contradict almost any preconception," he wrote. "There are Americans and South Vietnamese who can argue convincingly that the South Vietnamese army is generally brave or cowardly, that revolutionary development is beginning to succeed or continuing to fail, that bombing North Vietnam is advantageous or disadvantageous, that the United States is at the beginning of the end of the war or that no end is in sight."[166] Neither US nor South Vietnamese officials, Lowenstein observed, would admit to any such grey area. One example he cited: while the Viet Cong may have been succeeding in just 10 percent of the countryside, more than 60 percent of hamlets were deemed unsafe for elections. "The least that should have been done for the American decision makers and the American public," Lowenstein thought, "was to give both sides of the issue. But both sides were not being presented."[167]

The trip report that Lowenstein filed on his return from Vietnam remained confidential, a concession to Hart, who was not yet willing to go public with his newfound concerns about the war.[168] Hart, however, did share the report with Fulbright and Mansfield. Two weeks later, Fulbright went on record with his opposition to what he called "a hopeless venture." The war in Vietnam, he said, was "ruining our domestic and our foreign policy. I will not support it any longer."[169]

More Americans came to that conclusion after the Tet Offensive of January 1968, when North Vietnamese and Viet Cong forces staged a series of near-suicidal attacks on cities and installations across South Vietnam. In strictly military terms, the Tet Offensive marked a major defeat for the Communists, but it made a mockery of Johnson's claims of progress and it sapped much of the remaining US popular support for the war. A monetary crisis, driven by escalating costs of the Vietnam conflict, only added to the sense of doom bearing down on the Johnson White House.[170] Facing primary challenges from Eugene McCarthy and Robert Kennedy, Johnson announced on March 31 that he would no longer seek re-election. Richard Nixon, the longtime Republican hawk who nonetheless ran as a peace candidate with a "secret plan" to end the war, narrowly defeated the Democratic nominee, incumbent vice president Hubert Humphrey, in the November presidential election.

"Not Only Far from Won But Far from Over"

Nixon took office in January 1969 with the same goal as Johnson: to maintain an independent, non-Communist government in South Vietnam by neutralizing the Viet Cong and forcing the withdrawal of North Vietnamese forces. What was different was the strategy for achieving this objective. Nixon and his brilliant, strong-willed National Security Advisor, Henry Kissinger, emphasized the pacification of areas that were susceptible to Viet Cong control, a secret bombing campaign directed at North Vietnamese sanctuaries in neutral Cambodia, negotiation with Hanoi's paymasters—China and the Soviet Union, and the drawdown of American forces in favor of "Vietnamization" of the conflict. The United States, Nixon told the American people in a November 3 televised address, would no longer take the lead in fighting the North Vietnamese and the Viet Cong. Rather, American forces would train the army of South Vietnam (AVRN) to stand on its own. "Win the war by pulling out" was how Senator Albert Gore of Tennessee summed up the new strategy.[171] Nixon, faced with resurgent antiwar movement, appealed to a "silent majority" of Americans he believed was desperate to make good on the nation's bitter sacrifices, and he promised them his new strategy would result in "peace with honor."[172]

Of course, that support depended on the belief that Nixon was sincere in his pursuit of peace, a belief that Daniel Ellsberg no longer held. Ellsberg was one of the "whiz kids" who had been recruited to serve in the Pentagon during the Johnson administration, and he became an aide to Edward Lansdale, a retired Air Force major general and counterinsurgency specialist. He had met Lowenstein in Saigon in November 1967. He later resumed work at the RAND Corporation, where he was a consultant on a secret Defense Department study of the history of United States' involvement in Vietnam, starting in 1945. By the summer of 1969, however, he had become disaffected with the war in Vietnam. In October, he telephoned Lowenstein to say that he had in his possession a classified executive branch document that he wanted Fulbright to make public in hearings or on the Senate floor.[173]

Lowenstein went to Marcy, who arranged a meeting for Ellsberg with Fulbright, Lowenstein, Marcy, and Norvill Jones, counsel for the Senate Foreign Relations Committee. Seated on a sofa in Fulbright's office with two briefcases on the floor beside him, each containing the portions of the secret document he had copied, Ellsberg repeated his offer but did not describe the document beyond saying that it contained information wrongfully withheld from Congress. "He was not leaking anything," Marcy recalled. "He was trying to persuade the Committee, or Fulbright in particular, to ask for the historical compilation that was being put together." This was actually Ellsberg's second attempt to get the material into the public record. A few months earlier, he had given part of the document to Senator Charles Mathias, Jr., of Maryland, who had given it to Jones for safekeeping. Fulbright expressed interest in what Ellsberg had to offer, but in the end he decided not to pursue the matter, fearing that drawing on classified material leaked to Congress would jeopardize the Committee's credibility.[174] The portions of the document that Ellsberg had brought with him that day landed in the Committee safe along with the others and became important background for Lowenstein's later investigative work. Ellsberg would later give the document to the *New York Times*, which in 1971 published excerpts as "the Pentagon Papers."

Fulbright's hesitation over the Pentagon Papers did not signify any softening of his own opposition to the war. Since the first Vietnam hearings in 1966, he had emerged as one of the leading critics of US policy in Southeast Asia, which he saw as perpetuating the conflict.[175] But with broad support on the Senate Foreign Relations Committee for Nixon's strategy of disengagement, Fulbright no longer attacked the President's Vietnam policy as a whole, as he did with Johnson in office. For the moment at least, he assumed the role of the loyal opposition—content to chip away at the details of the policy in order to understand whether the administration's rosy assessments of Vietnamization were actually justified.[176]

Staff investigations would prove to be a powerful instrument to that end. In February 1969, Fulbright announced the formation of a new Ad Hoc Committee on United States Security Agreements and Commitments Abroad, to be chaired by Senator Symington. Investigators for the Symington subcommittee, Walter Pincus and Roland Paul, soon uncovered a clandestine war in Laos in which hundreds of US military advisers and CIA operatives had been directing Laotian forces in attacks on North Vietnamese enclaves. In follow-up hearings throughout the summer of 1969, Fulbright brandished excerpts from the report to harass witnesses and titillate the press. The Nixon administration's willful deception of Congress proved the point that Lowenstein had long been making to Fulbright: Congress could never hope to conduct effective oversight of the executive branch without its own source of information. It also gave some on the Senate Foreign Relations Committee reason to doubt what they were hearing about Vietnamization. So when Lowenstein proposed a fact-finding mission to Vietnam in late 1969, Fulbright agreed.[177]

Lowenstein teamed up with a new Committee staffer, Richard M. Moose, in what would prove to be an extraordinary partnership. Born and raised in Arkansas, Moose had been educated at the tiny Hendrix College in Conway, Arkansas, before going on to earn a Master's degree in international affairs at Columbia University. After joining the Foreign Service in 1956, he spent the next 10 years in Mexico City, Mexico; Yaounde, Cameroon; and Washington, DC before tiring of what he saw as the intellectually conformist, bureaucratic culture of the State Department. So he left to join the National Security Council, only to resign over disagreements with Kissinger. Moose was one of several Kissinger aides to have their telephones tapped by a Nixon White House eager to crack down on leaks.[178] In October 1969, he joined the staff of the Senate Foreign Relations Committee.[179]

Two such capable figures did not need any hand holding, Marcy recognized. "They were both former Department of State career officers. They were attuned to the kinds of things that I needed to know. I had implicit confidence in them."[180] Still, it was not that long ago that Roy Cohn and David Schine, aides to Joseph McCarthy, had abused the Senate's investigative authority by steering senators to conclusions that the aides themselves had reached. Lowenstein in particular was determined that Moose's and his work would remain above reproach, both in sources and methods. At Lowenstein's urging, Fulbright wrote to the Secretary of State, the Secretary of Defense, and the Director of the CIA requesting that Lowenstein and Moose receive full cooperation, which would include classified briefings, facilities in which to work and conduct interviews, and the freedom to go wherever they wished.[181]

The pair landed in Saigon on December 7 and settled in to the Hotel Caravelle.[182] During their six days in the South Vietnamese capital, they met with dozens of people, including the US ambassador Ellsworth Bunker; William Westmoreland's successor General Creighton Abrams, Jr.; US AID director Donald MacDonald; and numerous senior and junior diplomatic staff and military officers. They also heard from members of the Vietnamese government and the political opposition, foreign diplomats, and American and foreign correspondents.

Lowenstein and Moose did not limit themselves to Saigon. Traveling by helicopter, boat, and jeep for four and a half days, they traversed much of the country from Huế in the north and Dalat in the central highlands to Da Nang along the coast and the Mekong Delta in the south.[183] The impact of the war, they discovered, was uneven. In the north, the land looked prosperous. In the Delta, the war was ever-present, and in the vicinity of Route 1, described in Bernard Fall's *Street Without Joy*, they found large stretches of desolate countryside.

The investigators interviewed American military officers in English and Vietnamese military officers and province chiefs in French. With the help of interpreters, they also quizzed villagers about the progress of pacification efforts. One interpreter, an Army colonel with only a year of language training, asked highly scripted questions about the number of Viet Cong captured or killed, and concluded from the answers that the villagers were comfortable with their situation. That was hard to reconcile with the sound of mortar fire in the background, sporadic during the day and continuous at night. But another of their interpreters, an infantry officer named Jean Sauvageot, who was truly bilingual, got more accurate answers from the villagers. Dressed in civilian clothes, he asked open-ended questions— for example, "Is this village happy or sad?"—that delved deeper into the villagers' attitudes. "They seemed to be on edge, to have little hope for the future, and to have no faith in either the Communists or the Government," Lowenstein and Moose observed. Added Moose: "It was an extraordinary [perspective] that very few people would have had the opportunity to have…I always had the sense that I was hearing…as close to what was reality as far as the feelings of the people were concerned."[184]

Lowenstein and Moose wrote most of their report on a stopover at CINCPAC (the US Pacific Command in Pearl Harbor) and presented it to the Senate Foreign Relations Committee just before Christmas in 1969. In a process that would become standard for all their staff reports, they also negotiated with representatives from the Department of State, the Department of Defense, and the Central Intelligence Agency for a redacted, unclassified version that was made public on February 2, 1970.

Lowenstein and Moose emphasized that their goal was not "to characterize the glass as half empty or half full, but rather to describe the water level."[185] And in fact, they were careful not to offer predictions about the outcome of Vietnamization. Even so, their report, written in a tone that one journalist called "hopeful pessimism," could not have cheered anyone in the Nixon White House.[186] They described a general sense at all levels of the US military that pacification was working, but they questioned the validity of the indicators by which that progress was measured. In any case, progress depended on a large US advisory presence that the South Vietnamese Army most likely could not do without. "American advisers," they noted, "seem to be devoting little thought to working themselves out of their jobs." There was no leverage to be gained by Vietnamization if all Hanoi had to do was to wait until the United States withdrew and left the Saigon regime defenseless. Moreover, they argued, US policy rested on dubious assumptions with little evidence to support them: that the AVRN was up to the task of shouldering more of the war-fighting burden, that a weak South Vietnamese government could ever appeal to all major groups, and that Hanoi would stand by while the Americans built up the AVRN. Lowenstein ended the report by stating: "Dilemmas thus seem to lie ahead in Vietnam, as they have throughout our involvement in this war that appears to be not only far from won but far from over."[187]

That line was unexceptional in itself, but like much of the report, it directly contradicted the Nixon administration's central argument in favor of Vietnamization: that it would bring a speedy end to the war on American terms. It also reflected a judgment from within government itself—in this case, highly-regarded consultants working on behalf of the respected Senate Foreign Relations Committee. These attributes alone made the report newsworthy, but Marcy knew enough to submit the report on Friday for a Monday release.[188] Journalists, eager to leave for the weekend, pounced. All of a sudden, the story, with that one final sentence, was on the front page of every daily newspaper, in every wire service report, and on every nightly news broadcast. A sampling of headlines gives some sense of the extraordinary reaction generated by a single Congressional staff report: "War-Policy Basis Is Called Dubious" (*New York Times*); "Senate Study Questions Optimism on Viet War" (*Washington Post*); "2 Senate Probers Say Viet War Far From Over" (*Chicago Tribune*); "Vietnamization: Policy Under Fire" (*Time Magazine*); "Rosy Vietnam Reports Under Study" (*St. Louis Post Dispatch*); "New Dilemmas in Vietnam Foreseen" (*Philadelphia Inquirer*). Lowenstein and Moose also spoke to reporters on the condition that they would not be cited. They knew many of the reporters socially anyway. By becoming respected sources themselves, they further amplified the impact of the report.[189]

The Power of Information

The rash of publicity that greeted the Lowenstein/Moose staff report reflected a widespread hunger for the truth about the war in Vietnam after years of magical thinking and calculated deception. Fact-based while scrupulous in its avoidance of value judgments, the report earned praise from Fulbright and members of the Senate Foreign Relations Committee. George Kennan, with whom Lowenstein had shared a copy, praised Lowenstein's and Moose's work and shuddered over its implications. "I continue to feel that we have assumed an impossible task" in Vietnam, he wrote to Lowenstein, "and the sooner we admit and face the consequences, the better."[190] Marcy, acutely sensitive to the well-being of the Senate as an institution, may have been their toughest audience, but even he was convinced. "They did a beautiful job" with the first report, he said. "I was skeptical during the first mission, but by the second time they'd gone abroad, there was not much to be skeptical about."[191]

That second mission came in May 1970 following press reports that the Nixon administration was considering a request for military assistance from Cambodia's new leader, Lon Nol. Prince Sihanouk, who was overthrown in March, had given his tacit approval to the America's bombing North Vietnamese sanctuaries in eastern Cambodia after the *New York Times* and other media outlets had made the operation public in May 1969. Lowenstein himself had observed such approval in meetings between Mansfield and the prince in Phnom Penh in August 1969.[192] But Sihanouk was eager to keep his approval private, not wanting to be seen to supporting the American war in Vietnam, as that would violate his country's official neutrality. Lon Nol, on the other hand, was more openly friendly to the United States. This encouraged Nixon and Kissinger to consider more aggressive measures to prevent a Communist takeover in Cambodia that might imperil Vietnamization and the withdrawal of US troops from Vietnam.[193]

Lowenstein must have sensed this from comments by Secretary of State William P. Rogers in an April 27 appearance before the Senate Foreign Relations Committee, because he and Moose went to Fulbright's office immediately. "There is something going on out there and we think we should go" to Cambodia, they told Fulbright. Even the announcement of a trip, they argued, might keep the administration honest and prevent it from carrying out whatever it had planned.[194]

They were too late. On April 29, less than a week before Lowenstein and Moose arrived in Phnom Penh, South Vietnamese forces with American air support attacked enemy sanctuaries in Parrot's Beak, a strip of Cambodian territory 30 miles from Saigon. Two days later, US troops launched an assault on Fishhook, a North Vietnamese base 55 miles from Saigon. Nixon defended this action in an April 30 televised address, calling it an "incursion," not an "invasion," noting that Hanoi had already violated Cambodia's neutrality and therefore threatened the security of American troops in South Vietnam.

Lowenstein and Moose spent six days in Phnom Penh, providing daily updates to Fulbright and the Committee via classified cables from the US embassy. Joining combat troops aboard a military helicopter, they also visited the American and South Vietnamese areas of operation in Fishhook and Parrot's

Beak.[195] In their report, Lowenstein and Moose did not pass judgment on the legality of the Cambodian operation. Nor did they challenge the administration's policy of seeking to relieve pressure on the new Cambodian government. If the Lon Nol regime were to fail and be replaced by one that was friendly to Hanoi, they agreed, that would increase the threat to South Vietnam. Kissinger, in his memoir, would cite this observation as justification for the administration policy.

They did, however, dispute the timing of the incursion: Communist forces, far from amassing at the border for attacks on South Vietnam, were widely seen to be dispersing westward into Cambodia. "It appeared to us," they wrote, "that the United States and South Vietnamese military regarded Sihanouk's fall as an 'opportunity' to strike at enemy sanctuaries along the border." They noted the widespread view among military and diplomatic officials that the costs of the allied incursion had far outweighed its benefits. It made the Saigon regime, emboldened by its temporary success, less disposed to negotiate. By spreading South Vietnamese forces too thin, it left them more vulnerable to future attack. They also pointed out the larger implication of the incursion for US policy in Southeast Asia: Cambodia "has now been linked inextricably to the war in Vietnam, and…the terms of reference of that war have been permanently changed because its geographic area has been expanded."[196] A long-term military and economic assistance program for the Lon Nol government now seemed all but inevitable.

The Cambodian incursion infuriated many in Congress, who saw it as an illegal expansion of the war and, because it was an attack on a neutral country, a violation of the President's war-making powers. In the Senate, Fulbright began casting around for levers designed to tie the hands of the administration. He found one in a proposed amendment to the Special Foreign Assistance Act of 1971, sponsored by John Sherman Cooper, a Kentucky Republican, and Frank Church, an Idaho Democrat, that forbade the use of US ground troops or advisers in Cambodia. The amendment eventually passed in January

1971, though without limits on the use of air power, which allowed the bombing campaign to continue uninterrupted. In a symbolic act of defiance, Congress also voted to repeal the Tonkin Gulf Resolution, the main authorization for the war. Though Nixon would exploit loopholes in these and other legislative remedies, Congress would become increasingly assertive in trying to rein in Presidential power.[197]

The Cambodian incursion had exposed the limits of Congressional oversight—especially when Congress was confronted with an administration that had a penchant for secrecy and a contempt for Congress. The Senate Foreign Relations Committee received no information from the executive branch beyond what little they heard on request in executive session, and even this contained mostly data cherry-picked to support the administration's position. "The Committee didn't know what was going on," Moose said. "They got their information mainly out of the newspaper."[198] For example, Senator Case, a Republican on the Appropriations and Foreign Relations Committees, would have to learn about US funding of Thai forces in Laos from the *Christian Science Monitor*.[199]

Fulbright had been eloquent on the growing power imbalance between the legislative and executive branches. But the Nixon administration and its allies in Congress would never yield their advantage on the strength of rhetoric and logic alone. The Senate Foreign Relations Committee, Lowenstein and Moose argued, "will have to compel their respect and attention…We believe that better and more timely information is a large part of the answer."[200] And that, with Fulbright's blessing, was the focus of their work for the Committee over the next three years.[201]

In December 1970, as the Senate weighed a supplemental request for $255 million in military and economic assistance to Cambodia, Fulbright dispatched Lowenstein and Moose to Cambodia for another look.[202] Again, their report did not directly challenge the administration's policy in Cambodia. Some observers took Fulbright's decision to read the report into the Congressional record just before Christmas as an attempt to downplay its conclusions, but the report was later published as usual.[203] Nevertheless, Lowenstein and Moose confirmed how little had changed since the intervention of US and South Vietnamese forces six months earlier. The Cambodian government remained utterly dependent on US aid in order to hold Phnom Penh against enemy forces that controlled the countryside. The presence of enemy forces might also endanger the withdrawal of US troops from Vietnam. The price of Vietnamization, in other words, was the long-term aid program that Lowenstein and Moose had forecast after their first visit.[204]

For Lowenstein, however, the trip was memorable for a different reason. At a weekly cous-cous party given by the American press corps at the Golden Pagoda restaurant in Phnom Penh, someone had persuaded the chef to lace Lowenstein's food with hashish. Lowenstein spent the next 24 hours unconscious and woke up in the bathtub of his hotel room. This episode, wrote Joseph Alsop, the influential syndicated columnist and Vietnam hawk, proved that Lowenstein and Moose were a couple of drug addicts who couldn't be taken seriously.[205]

Shortly after his return from Cambodia, Lowenstein found himself with a minor role in one of the most emotionally wrenching issues of the conflict in Vietnam: the fate of thousands of American prisoners of war. The Nixon administration had failed in its attempts to secure the release of POWs held by Hanoi. These attempts included a failed rescue mission by US special forces. Fulbright, a staunch advocate for the families of POWs and MIAs, was one of several senators to have made repeated direct appeals to Hanoi to publish a list of POWs and repatriate the sick and wounded, but those too went unanswered.[206] Then, in December 1970, Fulbright and Senator Edward M. Kennedy of Massachusetts, along with Rennie Davis, head of the Committee of Liaison with Families of Servicemen Detained in North Vietnam, each received a telegram from the North Vietnamese mission in Paris. The message stated that if any one of them could send a representative to Paris in the next 24 hours, the mission would release the list of American prisoners of war.[207]

Lowenstein was in a Washington ski shop, outfitting his children for a family Christmas vacation, when he was summoned to the telephone. It was Marcy: Fulbright wanted Lowenstein to go to Paris. He rushed the children home to collect his passport and a toilet kit and boarded an evening flight to Paris. There, he met with Mai Van Bo, the head of North Vietnamese mission, who turned over the list of 339 POWs, including 20 who had died and 9 who had been released.[208] But Van Bo also reiterated Hanoi's position in the secret peace talks that Kissinger had arranged in February 1970, that despite Fulbright's entreaties, the release of prisoners would not be treated as a humanitarian issue. It would be connected to the withdrawal of US forces. Arriving back in Washington the following morning, Lowenstein delivered a summary of the meeting to Marcy, who forwarded the summary and the list of prisoners to Secretary of State William Rogers. It was the first time an authorized list had been provided to an American elected official. Rogers condemned Van Bo's providing the list as a "contemptible maneuver…for propaganda purposes."[209]

Other Lowenstein/Moose Investigations

The same moral conviction that led Fulbright to oppose the war and advocate for POWs also led him to take on the brutal military dictatorship in Greece, where, after seizing power in 1967, a junta promptly suspended the legislature, imposed martial law, and suppressed all dissent through imprisonment, torture, and execution. Since then, the regime had repeatedly pledged to restore democratic institutions and release political prisoners. The Nixon administration used these promises to justify its resumption of arms shipments to the junta, which had been suspended four years earlier, even as the need to maintain Greek military cooperation in NATO remained a paramount consideration. Suspicions grew on Capitol Hill that the US ambassador in Athens, Henry J. Tasca, had become too cozy with the colonels, weakening pressure on the regime to keep up its end of the bargain. In February 1971, Fulbright dispatched Lowenstein and Moose to investigate.[210]

Tasca dismissed the Senate inquiry as tantamount to interference in Greece's internal affairs and threw up every roadblock to Lowenstein and Moose's work, including a refusal to disclose to them a complete list of US military bases in Greece.[211] The investigators did manage to get cooperation from lower-level embassy staff who Lowenstein believed shared their misgivings over State Department policy.[212] With the help of foreign non-governmental organizations, including churches and charities, they also visited opposition leaders, many of them imprisoned. Often, they found themselves being shadowed by the Greek Military Police (ESA), who were on the CIA payroll.

The Lowenstein/Moose report pulled no punches, painting Tasca as an apologist for the junta. By taking colonels' statements at face value, the investigators argued, "the State Department had misled itself—and in the process Congress—about the willingness of the military junta in Athens to restore constitutional democracy in Greece." The embassy, they noted, "not only rationalizes the lack of progress but often appears to be more concerned with the regime's 'image' than with the substance of its actions."[213] The American policy of friendly persuasion, they concluded, had failed. Though Fulbright was ultimately unsuccessful in his attempts to cut off US aid to the junta, the Lowenstein/Moose report—by calling attention to the plight of political prisoners—had helped raise the morale of the regime's opponents, who feared that world concern and American concern for Greek democracy had faded.

The willingness of the Nixon administration to overlook human rights abuses in Greece in favor of perceived national security interests was a classic illustration of *realpolitik*: the belief that military and economic power, not moralism or legalism, determined great power relations. Lowenstein and

Moose observed a similar philosophy at work in Korea and the Philippines in November 1972, shortly after both countries had declared martial law. On a visit to Manila, the pair learned of a bizarre plot in which members of the political opposition had hired an American hit man to assassinate President Ferdinand E. Marcos. Their report referred to a "high Philippine government official" who tipped them off to the plot. That man was none other than Marcos himself. He insisted that the threat to his life had been his real reason for declaring martial law, and that he had refrained from revealing the plot earlier to avoid "undermining public confidence."[214]

Lowenstein and Moose found no such explosive revelations in Korea. This may have had something to do with the US ambassador, Philip Habib, whom both men knew and liked from previous assignments. When the two investigators landed in Seoul, they were met by a US embassy representative who took them directly to the ambassador's residence, refusing them a chance to shower and change after their long flight. "Now let me tell you something," said Habib, showing little wear from the heart attack that he had suffered in February, four months into his posting. "I didn't want you guys talking to anyone, including the maid in the hotel, until I got a hold of you. I don't care what you find out here. You're not going to find out anything that I don't know about."[215] Knowing Habib as they did, they expected he was right. They did, however, use their report to urge a review of US policy toward Korea. "With the U.S. involvement in Vietnam soon to be terminated, with the opening of North-South Korea talks, and with the end of our illusion about Korean democracy, it should be possible to take a fresh look at our residual interest in Korea." The refusal of the Nixon administration to take a position either for or against the preservation of democracy in Korea or the Philippines, they noted, had left the United States closely associated with authoritarianism. The nation's foreign policy appeared "to be in transition from the idealism of the past—based on an assumption that American democracy could and should be adopted by others—to a new pragmatism."[216]

A Never-Ending War

Nixon proved no more willing than his predecessors to make hard choices about the war in Vietnam. Obsessed with preventing the spread of Communism in Southeast Asia and deeply fearing defeat and humiliation, he launched a series of selective but dramatic escalations designed to buy time for Vietnamization to work.[217] In February 1971 he ordered a major clandestine ground operation in Laos. In a 12-day visit to Laos two months later, Lowenstein and Moose saw the extent of this commitment to Laotian forces. Out of $284 million in military aid in 1971, the United States had spent $70 million in CIA subsidies to operate a guerilla army. The pair saw these forces when they visited Long Tien, the principal guerilla base, and met with General Vang Pao, commander of the CIA-organized secret Hmong army. Lowenstein and Moose later discovered that the actual cost of CIA operations in Laos had routinely exceeded what had been requested from or reported to Congress.[218] At their suggestion, Senator Symington sponsored an amendment to a 1972 defense appropriations bill that established a $350 million ceiling on economic and military assistance to Laos, with the exception of US combat air operations over the Ho Chi Minh Trail in southern Laos.

Fresh off this modest victory, Lowenstein and Moose encouraged Fulbright to expand the Committee's inquiries into all military assistance programs, which they knew were often used as a cover for covert intelligence operations. Symington agreed, and in January 1972, Lowenstein and Moose returned to Southeast Asia for a comprehensive look at US-funded military activities in Laos, Thailand, and Cambodia.

The situation was a gloomy one. The United States was spending $100 million a year to equip, train, and support Thai irregulars in Laos in hopes of preventing a Communist takeover there, but fighting in Laos and Cambodia had only intensified. Laos was "closer to falling now than at any time in the past nine years," while Cambodia had "lost half its territory and is insecure in the remainder." Both countries were helpless pawns of the

United States, South Vietnam, and Thailand in their battle against the North Vietnamese. The administration apparently saw no alternative except "to continue to pursue the policies which thus far have served to intensify the destructive impact of the war while failing to arrest the deteriorating military, political, and economic situations in those two countries."[219] The findings of the report, which was made public in May 1972, prompted Symington to seek a delay in the military procurement bill for the following year "until the facts are brought out into the open. Otherwise, we become party to a deception which involves the use of public monies."[220]

Nixon, who was seeking to shore up support from the Republican party's right wing ahead of his fall reelection campaign, had already launched the sharpest escalation of the war since 1968. After North Vietnam's failed Easter Offensive, Nixon ordered B-52 bombing raids across the demilitarized zone into the Hanoi/Haiphong area, followed in May by mining Haiphong harbor and setting up a sea blockade of the north.[221]

Hanoi responded by softening its position in their negotiations with Kissinger. On May 8, Nixon proposed to withdraw all US forces within four months if North Vietnam released all POWs and agreed to an internationally supervised cease fire across Indochina. But could Saigon survive a cease-fire without massive US economic and military assistance? Presented with a $585 million aid request from the administration, Fulbright sent Lowenstein and Moose to Vietnam to find out.[222] They found a consensus among US officials was that the Easter Offensive, a massive invasion by the North Vietnamese, would have ended in defeat for the South Vietnamese if not for American air support. The investigators also uncovered a system in which the Defense Department had used different exchange rates for official and private transactions, resulting in an effective subsidy of $155 million to the Saigon government.[223] In a press conference following the report, Lowenstein noted that the "tremendous reliance" of South Vietnam on American support "raises doubts about whether the United States can withdraw. The South

Vietnamese have very little confidence in their own ability to face the future."[224]

Sixteen days before the 1972 election, Kissinger announced an armistice agreement with North Vietnam. This, along with Nixon's promise to replace the draft with an all-volunteer force and his continued drawdown of US troops, served to undercut his antiwar opponent, Senator George McGovern. Nixon was reelected with an overwhelmingly large popular vote margin.

After Saigon spurned Kissinger's peace agreement and Hanoi walked out of negotiations, the parties finally reached a settlement. Under the Paris Peace Accords, announced on January 27, 1973, the United States agreed to withdraw its remaining troops and advisers and dismantle all of its bases within 60 days, while North Vietnam agreed to release all US and other prisoners of war. The peace agreement, however, did not mean the immediate end of hostilities. Hanoi was allowed to keep its forces in the south, where it continued efforts to destabilize the Saigon government. The Nixon administration, seeking to shape postwar conditions on the ground, pressed its advantage with continuing air support and military assistance to local forces. As the chief Canadian delegate to the ceasefire commission said: "We came here to supervise a ceasefire. In fact, what we have been doing is observing a war."[225]

In April 1973, Lowenstein and Moose made their final visit to Vietnam to assess the extent of America's post-armistice commitment. They returned to Capitol Hill three weeks later in despair. "This massive tome should be entitled 'Everything you always wanted to know about Indochina but didn't have time to ask,'" they wrote to Marcy when they presented their report. "It represents eleven sleepless nights (out of the last eleven) and cost the committee about $10,000 in travel and living expenses. It reveals four secret wars (two old ones rediscovered and two new ones), at least four secret agreements, all manner of double entry bookkeeping, endless duplicity on the part of the Executive Branch, and the need for further field investigations—but never again in Indochina."[226]

They observed that in Vietnam, the North Vietnamese and the Viet Cong were determined to displace the Saigon government, while Saigon was unwilling to give the Communists any role in political life. An enduring peace was unlikely. In Laos, a cease-fire was holding, but only at a cost to the United States of $325 million in support for 17,000 Thai army troops and 18,000 Lao irregulars. And in Thailand, there was uneasiness about continuing intransigence from Hanoi and the prospect of the United States withdrawing and leaving its former allies in the region to fend for themselves.[227]

Their most significant finding, however, came in Phnom Penh. There they discovered that the US embassy was secretly directing air strikes against Khmer Rouge insurgents in clear violation of legislation intended to limit the involvement of US personnel in Cambodia. When the embassy continued to deny any role in the bombing, Lowenstein and Moose cabled Symington, who escalated the matter all the way to the President. Eventually, Nixon relented and Lowenstein and Moose received a briefing on Cambodian air operations.

The massive bombing campaign was designed to pressure the Khmer Rouge and its North Vietnamese supporters to sue for peace. But the level of fighting had increased after the air strikes began and was destined to continue "as long as [the US was] willing to defend from the air a Cambodian army that does not seem to be able to defend itself on the ground." Senator Symington announced in a press release accompanying the Lowenstein/Moose report that US policy was not "enforcing the peace" as Nixon had claimed, but was prolonging the war—"the beginning of another wasteful and immoral episode" in the long war in Indochina.[228]

The report's embarrassing revelation of an illegal US bombing campaign in the service of a civil war in Cambodia revived fears on Capitol Hill that America was being drawn into another Vietnam. In May, as the Watergate scandal weakened support for Nixon, the House of Representatives approved an antiwar amendment denying the administration's request to earmark funding for the bombing in Cambodia. The

Senate Foreign Relations Committee passed a Case-Church amendment to the 1973 State Department budget that prohibited further direct military action in Indochina unless specifically authorized by Congress. The amendment was approved the following month by veto-proof margins in both houses.[229]

Lowenstein and Moose produced one final staff report, a study of America's European security commitments. It must have come as a relief from the drama of Southeast Asia. The report focused on the US nuclear posture in Europe, where some 7,000 weapons were spread out across more than 100 installations. Although the public version was heavily censored, with fewer than half of its 27 pages left intact, it nonetheless provided the fullest public accounting to date of the deployment and doctrine of use for nuclear weapons in Europe. Two-thirds of those weapons were allocated to Allied forces, but all were kept in the custody of the United States, their exact whereabouts unknown even to European leaders. This merely underscored the extent to which Europeans were hostage to American decisions, and thus to American politics.[230]

Persistence, Perseverance, and Opportunity

In all, Lowenstein and Moose produced 11 staff reports, logging tens of thousands of miles in the process. They enjoyed a rare intellectual rapport that made forming conclusions and writing them up straightforward. Each would draft a section of a report that the other would edit. "There wasn't any substantive disagreement," Lowenstein said. "We saw things exactly the same way, presented them exactly the same way, and that's what made it possible to do those reports as quickly as we did them."[231] The two men complemented one another in other key aspects. After several years on the Senate Foreign Relations Committee staff, Lowenstein knew his way around Capitol Hill, while Moose, a former NSC staffer, knew how to interpret the information they received from the White House. They were a bit of an odd couple: the balding, cigar-smoking Lowenstein with an Ivy League manner, and the country-bred Moose with his easy Arkansas patter. Moose could talk to people that the more polished Lowenstein could not reach. Recalled Lowenstein, "If we were out in Vietnam or Cambodia and a helicopter pilot was from down south, Dick was on the case. He could get more out of the guy in five minutes than I could in five years."[232] Even *Newsweek* contrasted the two, describing Lowenstein as exuding "the quiet capability of a Park Avenue psychiatrist" and Moose as looking like "a slightly mod Civil War cavalry officer."

Lowenstein and Moose's security clearances gave them access to classified information, but this was a small part of their success. They were doing investigative reporting of very high order—"a remarkable piece of journalism," as *The Evening Star* said of their second Cambodia report. The inner workings of the US bombing campaign in Cambodia, US support for the military dictatorship in Greece, the assassination plot against Philippine President Ferdinand Marcos, the first authoritative account of US nuclear weapons in Europe—revelations like these, observed journalist and historian Stanley Karnow, "would have earned them Pulitzer prizes had they been newsmen."[233]

The pair had a nose for facts, which they often found in the public domain. From data on Defense Department appropriations to executive branch testimony before Congress, they accumulated a vast amount of raw material that was readily available to anyone who bothered to look for it.[234] Wherever they traveled, they also pocketed every piece of documentation they could lay their hands on: slides, leaflets, notices—anything that might reveal discrepancies when compared to what they heard in a briefing with an ambassador or senior military officer.

They scoured their networks and talked to journalists in the know. Moose, who had worked in the White House press office, looked to Laurence Stern of the *Washington Post* and Emerson

Chapin of the *New York Times*. Lowenstein had become friendly with reporters assigned to cover the Senate Foreign Relations Committee: Ned Kenworthy and John Finney of the *Times* and Spencer Rich of the *Post*, as well as Stanley Karnow. Lowenstein's comments to them, though always cited as an anonymous source and always given with Marcy's permission, earned him favors he could redeem for information on the Nixon White House and the military chain of command.[235] With their connections in the Senate, Lowenstein and Moose also could call on prominent academics to bolster their findings, including those at the Federation of American Scientists for arms control matters and the School of Advanced International Studies at Johns Hopkins for regional questions.

Inside information and subject-matter expertise were a critical combination. Official briefings with embassy and military staff, Lowenstein recalled, turned out to be "much more informative than one would have thought if you knew what you were talking about." As Kissinger, then National Security Advisor, told Moose about the classified cables from their first trip to Cambodia: "No one can say that you and Lowenstein did not know the right questions to ask!" Lowenstein, with his background as a former naval officer and staff member of the Naval War College, had a good ear for military euphemism. "All kinds of things were said that were so obviously not true that you could tell what was being covered up."[236]

What gave the Lowenstein/Moose reports their real force, however, were the perspectives they got from people on the ground. Through interviews with everyone from local villagers and opposition leaders to junior embassy and military officers, the investigators were able to see the gaps between policies created in conference rooms and their effects in practice. Foreign Service officers in the provinces of Vietnam were candid about the challenges America faced in Southeast Asia. "The farther you got from Saigon," Moose recalled, "the more pessimism you ran into. The further down the hierarchy you got, the more realism you encountered."[237] Even when embassy staff agreed with US policy, many were willing to offer honest observations out of a conviction that the legislative branch was entitled to the facts.[238]

Relationships with junior military officers, in particular, paid dividends. Lowenstein and Moose obtained much of their data for their first Cambodia report from Charles F. Meissner, a captain in the US Army at the US Military Assistance Command (MACV) who had a PhD from the University of Wisconsin and knew more about what was going on in Cambodia than most of his superior officers.[239] Conversations with second lieutenants in Huế, on their first trip to Vietnam in December 1969, tipped them off to a rash of attacks by American soldiers on superior officers and noncommissioned officers—200 in 1970 alone.[240] These incidents became known as "fragging," after the fragmentation grenades that were often the prime weapon.

Perhaps the most valuable asset Lowenstein and Moose brought to their investigations was persistence. They always had to run an obstacle course set by US military and embassy staff who were determined to run out the clock on their requests for information. "By the time you get from your hotel to the airport, take a two-hour helicopter ride to the local military headquarters, sit through a briefing that lasts for an hour and a half, have lunch with the general that lasts another hour, get back on the helicopter, go back into Saigon and get back to your hotel, a day has gone."[241] Lowenstein and Moose were not so easily sidetracked. "They couldn't outlast us because we were there for weeks at a time."[242] This proved invaluable, because as Lowenstein said, "if you have a lot of time, accidents will happen."[243]

In fact, much of what Lowenstein and Moose uncovered in their travels was a matter of luck, although clearly they had a knack for being in the right place at the right time. Ahead of their May 1972 visits to Thailand, Laos, and Cambodia, they stumbled on to a previously unnoticed Voice of America interview in which Laotian premier Souvanna Phouma all but confirmed that the battalions of Thai "volunteers" operating in Laos were not volunteers at all, in violation of a recent legislative prohibition on the use of defense funds to support third-party forces operating there or in Cambodia.[244] Later that year, on their way back from Korea and the Philippines in November, Lowenstein and Moose stopped at the US embassy in Paris, where they were supposed to be briefed on the Vietnam negotiations. They were deposited in an empty office. Looking for a notepad, Moose opened a desk drawer and discovered a telegram with an account of the previous day's negotiating session between Washington and Hanoi. There, in the telegram, were the details of a secret protocol in which Nixon promised $3.25 million in aid for postwar reconstruction. That aid had never been communicated to Congress, and a week after Moose and Lowenstein reported it to the Committee, Fulbright called Nixon to offer advice on how to administer the aid that nobody was supposed to know about.[245]

The most dramatic illustration of happenstance was the discovery of illegal US air operations in Cambodia. Embassy staff in Phnom Penh had been evasive in response to Lowenstein and Moose's questions about the nature and extent of the bombing campaign. Lowenstein and Moose's suspicions were further aroused when an embassy air attaché confided that he had more information that he was forbidden to reveal to them.[246] Then Moose happened to drop by the local United Press International (UPI) office to check the baseball scores on the news ticker. There he found Sylvana Foa, a correspondent for UPI and *Newsweek*.

Foa was considered one of the most dogged journalists, earning the enmity of the US Embassy for reporting on US government misdeeds. She went on to become foreign editor of UPI and eventually the first woman to serve as spokesperson for the United Nations Secretary General.

Foa was sitting in the UPI office with a cheap transistor radio receiver pressed to her ear. "Do you want to hear something interesting?" she asked. On the radio were the voices of American F-111 and B-52 pilots and an American air controller. Given the radio's limited range, the signal could not be coming from across the border in Thailand. It had to be coming from Phnom Penh. "We knew from all of our experience in dealing with air operations in other places what the call signs meant," Lowenstein later explained. "[T]he US embassy was directing the [warplanes]."[247]

Denied information from the Pentagon on the number of sorties flown by US bombers over Laos and Cambodia, Lowenstein and Moose found help on a stopover at CINCPAC in Pearl Harbor on the way home. Over dinner one night, they heard about a fellow visiting from Washington who "plays computers the way Paderewski plays the piano." So they went to see him. The technician, it turned out, was using CINCPAC's mainframe computer to log every American sortie flown in Southeast Asia. The two asked innocently, "Well, as a test case, how many sorties were flown in Laos last month?" CINCPAC was apparently not aware that the Pentagon had declared this information off-limits to Lowenstein and Moose because the computer soon spit out a map with every sortie in Laos and Cambodia—when the pilot took off, his destination, his mission, and when he landed. This data became the basis of their report on US air operations in Cambodia.[248]

Their dogged search for the facts about US policy throughout Southeast Asia earned Lowenstein and Moose the respect of professional journalists.[249] Even some in the Nixon administration recognized them as capable and honest critics. As Winston Lord, Kissinger's top assistant on the secret negotiations with North Vietnam, said of their reports: "Yes, this complicates the administration's efforts, but it's…patriotic, non-partisan, analytical, not some outraged screed" of the kind he saw coming from the antiwar movement.[250]

Lord later revealed that, in a somewhat whimsical homage to Lowenstein, he had used "Lowenstein" as his code name as he and fellow diplomats moved from one Paris safe house to another during the secret negotiations with the North Vietnamese. His rationale was that Lowenstein was well-known in the administration for his desire to end the war, and his name began with an "L."²⁵¹ Lord went on to become president of the Council on Foreign Relations and US ambassador to China.

Lord's State Department colleague, deputy Secretary of State John N. Irwin II, who later became US ambassador to France, expressed a view similar to Lord's in a 1972 cable to ambassadors and senior military personnel stationed at US embassies. While warning them to be prepared for an "adversarial" approach from Lowenstein and Moose, he also praised the two as "highly knowledgeable and well-prepared" and "more sophisticated and more understanding of foreign relations" than other Congressional investigators he had encountered.²⁵²

Taken together, the staff reports that Lowenstein and Moose produced from 1969 to 1973 played a vital role at a unique moment in history. They brought to light information that the executive branch would not give Congress, enabling Fulbright and the Senate Foreign Relations Committee to hold the Nixon administration to account. By exposing the limits of American power, they also corrected false hopes and false claims about the war in Southeast Asia. For Fulbright, they validated his premise that by educating people through staff reports and hearings, he could shape public opinion.²⁵³

The Lowenstein/Moose reports did something else too. By taking back some of the information power that had passed to the executive branch, they empowered Congress to reassert its institutional prerogatives, long before Watergate triggered a larger backlash against the untrammeled power of the imperial presidency.²⁵⁴

Ulysses S. Grant put the presidential stamp on Long Branch
By acquiring a large seaside cottage, driving his carriage
Along the beach and returning every summer of his presidency.
Postcard of the Grant cottage at Elberon, New Jersey. c. 1914

Joan Schnorbus, Long Branch Historical Museum Association

The New York Times
Published: December 4, 1893

Gen. Grant's Cottage Sold.
LONG BRANCH, N.J., Dec. 3.--The Grant cottage, in Elberon, has been sold to Mrs. E. S. Price of New-York, who has occupied it during the past three Summers. It is understood that Mrs. Grant received $33,000 for the property. The cottage was presented to Gen. Grant in 1869 by George W. Childs, ex-Collector Thomas Murphy, Gen. Horace Porter, and others. It was occupied by the Grant family for several Summers.

Snowbound between Trieste and Ljubljana, 1950

With liaison officer Albert Finci on the stairs of the Ministry of Justice building in Sarajevo, 1951

Observing food aid distribution in Bosnia, 1951

Official Navy photograph at commissioning as Ensign, April 1952

With Senator Church (left) leaving the Foreign Ministry in London, May 1966

With US Ambassador Godley (center) in the field in Laos, 1971

With Senator Fulbright

With Senators Fulbright (second from left) and
Church (third from left) at a Committee hearing

FINDING THE FACTS WITH L & M

Their plots don't titillate and their writing doesn't swing. They have never even been at the bottom of the bestseller list, much less at the top. But coauthors James Lowenstein and Richard Moose have an impressive audience. As globe-trotting fact finders for the Senate Foreign Relations Committee, their studies have become must reading for anyone seriously interested in American foreign policy. Over the past four years, they have documented the U.S.'s "secret war" in Laos, revealed the workings of the U.S. bombing campaign in Cambodia and examined U.S. support for the dictatorship in Greece. Last week there was another L & M moment as Lowenstein and Moose published their latest report on Indochina.

Like several earlier efforts, the new study scrutinizes the tangled web of America's Asian involvement. Though U.S. troops and POW's have come home from Indochina, the two Senate staffers report, Washington is still heavily engaged in the area. There are 44,000 U.S. troops in Thailand. In Cambodia, the U.S. is footing the bill for tens of thousands of native troops who don't exist. As for South Vietnam, though the Nixon Administration is successfully shoring up President Nguyen Van Thieu with millions of dollars and some 8,000 American "civilian" advisers, Lowenstein and Moose are pessimistic about the chances of any long-range settlement. These days, they point out, "the U.S. is in no position to press President Thieu on political matters."

Raw Materials: If all this is less than cheering news, it is at least well documented. To compile their study, L & M made a grueling three-week trip to Asia in April—their ninth in four years. Their assignment: to provide the Senate Foreign Relations Committee, which is frequently in the dark thanks to White House secrecy, with the raw materials for foreign-policy decision making. And there is no question that the pair succeeds in doing just that. "They have a nose for facts," Sen. Stuart Symington told NEWSWEEK'S Lloyd Norman last week, "and they have been able to find out a lot we did not know." Adds one admiring newsman: "They cut through government cover-up and get the real story."

Getting the real story is far from easy. Each trip is preceded by weeks of boning up with government and academic sources. Once on-scene, they act more like probing journalists than government officials. In briefings and interviews that begin at breakfast and often continue far into the night, Lowenstein and Moose question American military and embassy personnel, foreign diplomats, officials of the host government—and the opposition.

They also get a lot of help from U.S. newsmen—sometimes of the unsolicited variety. "When we were in Phnom Penh in December 1970," Lowenstein recalls, "we were invited by some newspaper people to a couscous dinner. The couscous was laced with some stuff that looked like parsley but turned out to be hashish...I couldn't write my name for two days."

Moose: Orders on the radio

individuals. At 45, the balding, cigar-smoking Lowenstein exudes the quiet capability of a Park Avenue psychiatrist, and his diplomatic, Ivy League manner puts high-level officials at ease. The 41-year-old, Arkansas-bred Moose, by contrast, looks like a slightly mod Civil War cavalry officer—and by his own admission his manner is a mite more blunt.

One trait the two men share is a passion for exercise. Lowenstein recently flew to Paris for a tennis tournament (he reached the quarter-finals), while Moose has just backpacked the Appalachian Trail. Thanks to the Foreign Relations Committee, however, there is not much time for hobbies. "Lowenstein and Moose are the committee's antennae," says one Washington official. And where will their next assignment take them? In the words of committee chairman Sen. J. William Fulbright: "Where the trouble is."

During their mission to Cambodia this spring, the U.S. Embassy tried to call a halt to their prying. At first, embassy officials in Phnom Penh refused Lowenstein and Moose a briefing on U.S. bombing. When a local newswoman loaned them her radio receiver—tuned to the frequency on which the embassy was directing the air missions—they quickly cabled their findings to Senator Symington, who took the news to none other than the Secretary of State. "At the time," Moose reports, "even the State Department didn't realize the full extent of the embassy's bombing role."

Teamwork: Nothing in their background pegged L & M as budding detectives. Both served in the Foreign Service before signing on as $32,000 Senate consultants, and only since teaming up in 1969 have they developed the prodigious fact-gathering capacity and flair for close teamwork that they now display. Despite their joint endeavors they are very different

Lowenstein: Hash in the couscous

Photos by Lawrence McIntosh

At the White House with Deputy CIA Director Frank Carlucci, National Security Adviser Zbigniew Brzezinski, and President Carter, January 1977

Oath of Office as Ambassador to Luxembourg with daughter Laurinda holding the Bible, 1977

Greeting the Marshall of the Grand Ducal Court with Madame de Muyser, daughter Laurinda, and the Embassy DCM J. D. Phillips, 1977

With Marine Guard detachment at the Embassy in Luxembourg, 1977

With Luxembourg Prime Minister Gaston Thorn, 1979

With Luxembourg Foreign Minister Colette Flesch, 1979

The American team at the Lux-Am plate, 1979

With brothers Hugh and Peter and mother, 1990

Back in Bosnia, 1997

With former Ceylon (Sri Lanka) Prime Minister Dudley Senanayake and longtime friend Bradman Weerakoon

With friend Pierre de Gunzburg 60 years after first meeting, 2010

With former French Ambassador to the U. S.
Francois Bujon de l'Estang 41 years after first meeting, 2010

Presiding at the trophy for the Seal Harbor Club championships won by son Price and grandson Jake, with tennis committee chairman Tim Clark, 2013

With French American Foundation France Chairman Jean-Luc Allavena and former French president Giscard d'Estaing at a gala celebrating the formation of the Foundation, 2015

With former Secretary of State Henry Kissinger at a French American Foundation gala in New York

With Bill Weathers at the 90 clay court singles nationals, 2017

4 Return to State

Kissinger's State Department

At the end of 1973, Marcy retired as chief of staff of the Senate Foreign Relations Committee. His capable deputy, Pat Holt, replaced him. The Committee staff was nonetheless deprived of a formidable administrator whose deep experience and connections throughout Washington had amplified the influence of the Lowenstein/Moose reports.

This was one of the reasons Lowenstein began to reconsider his position on the Committee staff, but there were others. His two children were entering their adolescent years, and overseas travel was taking its toll on his family life. Lowenstein was also thinking seriously of leaving public service for the private sector, with business school a logical next step. He had approached the Committee two years earlier about sponsoring him for Harvard's 13-week Advanced Management Program, which was geared to mid-career executives like him. But Mansfield, whose own staffer Charlie Ferris had attended the program, poured cold water on the idea. "I think Lowenstein is one of the most superb members of the staff that I know of," he said. "I don't think that he would learn anything. I think that he would teach the faculty at Harvard a good deal that they know nothing about."[255] Nevertheless, Lowenstein remained convinced that adding management training to his experience in foreign affairs would open up interesting opportunities in the corporate world, and that now was the time to revisit the business school option.

When he went to Fulbright to announce his plans, Fulbright stopped him. "Well, I'm seeing Kissinger tomorrow. Do you want me to ask him whether he would like to have you back in the Foreign Service?" Kissinger had been impressed with the staff reports that Lowenstein and Moose had produced, even though they often countered the strategy he and Nixon were pursuing in Southeast Asia. Lowenstein himself knew from people who worked with Kissinger that his reports were on the Secretary's desk the morning they were released.[256]

At about that time, Lowenstein had dinner with his friend Arthur Hartman, whom he had known during his Marshall Plan days in Paris and with whom had worked at the State Department's Bureau of European Affairs (EUR) in the late 1950s. Lowenstein had kept in touch with Hartman in Brussels in the early 1970s, when Hartman was deputy chief of mission at the US mission to the European Communities.

Hartman had recently been named Assistant Secretary of State for European Affairs and he invited Lowenstein to become one of his deputies.[257] Lowenstein's appointment met with some resistance from hawks and hardliners in the State Department, who bristled at the notion of welcoming back someone they believed was a dove on Vietnam. In the White House, Peter Flanigan, an investment banker and fundraiser who had become an influential aide to Nixon, put up a fuss. Even Lowenstein confessed some surprise at being brought back. But with a nudge from Lawrence Eagleburger, his former colleague at the Embassy in Belgrade and now a key Kissinger assistant, the appointment was pushed through before more opposition could take hold, and Lowenstein was sworn in at a quiet administrative ceremony.[258]

As he said his good-byes to the Senate Foreign Relations Committee, Lowenstein expressed pride in what the

Committee had been able to achieve over the past nine years, both for the Senate as an institution and for the country as a whole. "I feel strongly about the question of independent reporting and fact finding," he wrote Symington, "and I am convinced that without it the Senate will never be able to play an effective role in the field of foreign affairs." He offered the same views to Fulbright. Under Fulbright's leadership, he wrote the senator, the Committee had "saved this country from following courses of action which would have altered the balance in our system of government in fundamental and harmful ways."[259] Two months later, Fulbright, who had spent 30 years in the Senate, would lose his primary race to Arkansas governor Dale Bumpers, who capitalized on widespread disillusionment with Congress.

Moose eventually returned to the State Department much later. It was bitter disagreements with Kissinger at the National Security Council in 1969 that had led him to Capitol Hill in the first place. He remained for two more years on the staff of the Senate Foreign Relations Committee and went on to produce four more staff reports, this time with Charles F. Meissner, Lowenstein and Moose's contact at MACV. Meissner later unfortunately perished in Croatia in the 1996 plane crash that also claimed the life of Secretary of Commerce Ron Brown.[260]

Lowenstein joined the State Department as the number two deputy assistant secretary in the Bureau of European Affairs (EUR), behind Wells Stabler, the principal deputy. It marked a return to the bureau where he had last served under Lane Timmons in the late 1950s and early 1960s. His main duties revolved around multinational European institutions, including NATO and the European Community. He also represented EUR in meetings with foreign ambassadors.

Lowenstein's early months back at State were consumed by a crisis in Cyprus. After Cypriote troops backed by Greek army officers overthrew the Cyprus government in July 1974, Turkey invaded northern Cyprus. Much of the American response fell to Hartman and Joe Sisco, whose shuttle diplomacy over the next months was aimed at preventing a second invasion and reaching some accommodation between Greece and Turkey, two NATO allies.

When news of the Turkish invasion broke, Lowenstein had just arrived in Maine for a brief vacation, but was immediately called back to Washington. He went to work on the State Department's operational response, which helped to protect American citizens on the island, but his work on the Senate Foreign Relations Committee disqualified him from taking any active role in resolving the crisis. As the author of a staff report that was highly critical of the military junta in Greece, he was not seen as a neutral party, and his superiors thought it better that he stay out of the fray.[261] He could take some satisfaction, however, in knowing that the Turkish invasion of Cyprus forced the Greek army colonels from power, leading to the restoration of democracy in Greece. [262]

In February 1975, after Wells Stabler was named ambassador to Spain, Lowenstein became principal deputy assistant secretary. This meant that he was acting assistant secretary whenever Hartman was out of the country, which was often. Hartman said, "Assistant Secretaries' lives are hell, between the traveling and the meetings...and doing all the things the Secretary of State does not wish to do, as well as serving him; I think it is the hardest job I ever had, but the most fun."[263] Lowenstein also attended many of Kissinger's daily morning meetings in his capacity as acting assistant secretary. Kissinger was exacting, and Lowenstein rose at 5:30 in the morning in order to get to the State Department and read the overnight cables before the 8 am meeting.[264]

It was as a stand-in for Hartman that Lowenstein headed an orientation for new US ambassadors—including Kingman Brewster, who had been appointed US ambassador to the Court of St. James. Brewster was a former professor at Harvard Law School and had taught a course on agency law that Lowenstein, as a student, did not remember fondly. It turned out that neither did Brewster. "That was the worst experience of my academic life," he told Lowenstein. "I'd appreciate it if you never mention it again." When they met again in London a couple of years later, Brewster was diplomatic. "Mr. Lowenstein and I have had a previous relationship but neither us is at liberty to discuss it."[265]

Lowenstein also stood in for Hartman at a black-tie dinner held in honor of the Netherlands prime minister, Joop M. den Uyl, at the White House on May 14, 1975. There was some commotion as Kissinger and Donald Rumsfeld, the Defense Secretary, were running in and out of the room throughout the dinner. Lowenstein turned to Navy Secretary J. William Middendorf, who was seated next to him, and said "There must be something going on." Middendorf replied: "Beats me. I have no idea what's going on." Only later that evening, listening to the radio on the drive home, did Lowenstein learn what had happened. Two days earlier, Khmer Rouge forces had seized the US merchant vessel SS *Mayaguez* and its crew off the coast of Cambodia. At the time of the dinner, President Ford and his advisors were organizing an operation involving a Navy frigate and the US Marines to rescue the *Mayaguez* crew. Through it all, no one had thought to inform Secretary Middendorf, the official responsible for the Navy.

Kissinger was an extremely complex figure. He ran the State Department with an iron fist and insisted that assistant secretaries and their deputies, which included Lowenstein, draft daily talking points for him lest they stray from official policy. Recalled L. Paul Bremer, one of Kissinger's aides: "It was a mechanism which only a megalomaniac like Henry, who worked that hard, could actually do."[266] Kissinger was prone to tantrums too, and could be cruel and manipulative to the point of sadism.[267] These traits did not bother Lowenstein for the most part. He tolerated Kissinger's heavy-handed management style, and never took his ranting and raving personally; if anything he found Kissinger amusing.[268]

Lowenstein did find the Secretary to be secretive, and at times devious. When Kissinger's aide, Helmut ("Hal") Sonnenfeldt, had Lowenstein set up a dinner for Kissinger and Olivier Chevrillon, editor of *Le Point*, in Paris, he made Lowenstein go to extraordinary lengths to keep the meeting from the US ambassador, Jack Irwin, and the embassy staff. On another occasion, ahead of flights to several US embassies in Europe, Lowenstein was asked to arrange Kissinger's schedule at one embassy so that Kissinger would have no time to meet with the ambassador. When the ambassador later greeted Kissinger on the airport tarmac and expressed disappointment that they would have no time to meet, the Secretary feigned incredulity: "What? I specifically asked Lowenstein to make sure there was time in the schedule for us to meet!"[269]

Another episode involved the US ambassador to Yugoslavia, Laurence Silberman. Convinced that the United States was coddling Yugoslavia's leader, Marshal Josep Broz Tito, at the expense of American credibility, Silberman had repeatedly ignored all policy directives from the State Department. Tensions came to a head over his handling of a naturalized American citizen, Laszlov Toth, who had been arrested and imprisoned by the Yugoslav secret police. Hartman, with Kissinger's approval relayed through Eagleburger, sent Lowenstein to Belgrade to read Silberman the riot act. "So how do you fellows think I'm doing?" Silberman asked when he and Lowenstein sat down together. Lowenstein proceeded to go through his talking points until Silberman brandished a telegram from Kissinger he had received two days earlier. "Dear Larry, I just want you to know I think you're doing a fantastic job out there, and I'm full of admiration." "Typical Kissinger," said Lowenstein. Silberman looked at Lowenstein and replied, "Why don't you go off and play tennis with my DCM [deputy chief of mission]?" which is what Lowenstein did."[270] Lowenstein would go on to become friends with the DCM, Brandon Sweitzer, who eventually became president of the insurance brokerage Marsh and one of Lowenstein's consulting clients after his retirement.[271]

Kissinger attracted an extraordinarily talented, dedicated group of people, including Hartman, Bremer, Roy Atherton, Lawrence Eagleburger, Thomas Enders, Phil Habib, Winston Lord, Joseph Sisco, and George Vest. Almost without exception they were career Foreign Service officers, and many had

National Security Council experience too, which gave Kissinger a good mix of advice. Bremer described them as "the strongest group of assistant secretaries since Dulles had been Secretary." For many of them, working in such a group would be a highlight of their careers. Lord found his tenure as assistant secretary "exhilarating and exciting," while Sisco remembered his to be "the best job I ever had in the State Department."[272]

Lowenstein also had high praise. As a group, he recalled, Hartman and the other assistant secretaries and their deputies "were competent, efficient, no nonsense, open to being persuaded, and with no back-stabbing"—remarkable for any bureaucracy.[273] And while he found the State Department somewhat parochial after nine years with the Senate Foreign Relations Committee, the impact of his work was potentially much greater.[274]

Forming the French-American Foundation

A lifelong Francophile, Lowenstein had long been dismayed by the Francophobia he encountered both inside and outside of government. To most in Congress and the State Department, the French could do no right. A similar antagonism pervaded the press. The French, meanwhile, seemed to exhibit a reflexive anti-Americanism. Such tensions were not new: France and the United States had a long history of petty squabbles dating back to the early years of their alliance. French arms and money helped the United States prevail against the British in the American Revolutionary War, but before the eighteenth century was over, American frigates were battling French privateers throughout the West Indies in an undeclared war against Napoleon's navy. The French-American relationship seemed to have grown more fraught in recent years, as Americans grew impatient with Gaullist ambition, and differences hardened over vexing issues such as decolonization of the developing world, nuclear arms, and the war in Indochina. At a Council on Foreign Relations meeting,

Lowenstein wondered aloud to James Chace, managing editor of the Council's journal *Foreign Affairs*, whether something might be done to soften attitudes between the French and Americans and put the relationship on a more rational footing.

As it happened, Chace had been having similar conversations with Nicholas Wahl, a noted historian of French politics at Princeton, and he introduced Lowenstein and Wahl in late 1973. The two knew there were many US nonprofits focused either on French language and French culture or on relations between the United States and Europe as a whole. The French-American relationship, they thought, was unique—"a case study in mutual misperceptions" that called for a different approach. Their idea was to form a non-governmental organization devoted to the bilateral relationship between France and the United States—a forum for serious people to engage on political and economic issues and policy.[275]

Such an enterprise, of course, would require funding and support not just in the United States but also in France, where active French participation was needed to give credibility to any organization involved in discussing bilateral policy issues. "This would not be yet another case of Americans dealing with the French (or preaching to the French) without some sort or reciprocity," Lowenstein said. Rather than a New York- or Washington-based organization with a satellite office in Paris, Lowenstein and Wahl saw the enterprise as two independent foundations with the same name, each with its own board. Each board would accommodate the idiosyncrasies of the particular partner.[276]

The next step was to test the waters in Paris. In October 1974, Lowenstein and Wahl had lunch with Emmanuel (Bobbie) de Margerie, the director of Western European affairs at the Quai d'Orsay and a future ambassador to London and Washington, who immediately threw his support behind their plan for dual foundations. Lowenstein made sure he had the blessing of Assistant Secretary of State for European Affairs Arthur Hartman. Hartman, in turn, made sure that the US embassy in Paris gave its backing to the project. Indeed, the embassy helped to arrange a pivotal meeting for Lowenstein and Wahl with Claude Pierre-Brosolette, chief of staff of French president Valéry Giscard d'Estaing. Pierre-Brosolette, said de Margerie, was "very responsive and enthusiastic and said that he was certain that the newly elected French President would approve of such an idea."

In April 1975, Lowenstein and Wahl pitched their idea to a group of French government officials, academics, and business people at a dinner organized by Jean Pierre Soisson, the Secretary of State for Universities and a confidante of the French president. They agreed that the French foundation, like its American counterpart, should be strictly nonpartisan; that a board in France of broad professional composition should run it; that it should be formally inaugurated as part of America's bicentennial year, 1976; and, most importantly, that the French organization could not be brought into being without government funds. Jean Laloy, Director of Cultural Affairs at the Quai d'Orsay, later agreed to provide the necessary seed money. David McGovern, the managing partner of Shearman and Sterling's Paris office who was a friend and Yale classmate of Lowenstein, agreed to do the necessary legal work pro bono to establish the French Foundation. His colleague Edward Tuck, a partner in the firm's New York office, would do the same for the American organization.

With arrangements for the French foundation in place, Lowenstein and Wahl turned their attention to the American entity. In May 1975, they organized two dinners, one in Washington and one in New York, to gauge American support for the prospective organization. The consensus that emerged was that the two foundations should be linked by a common name, a parallel legal structure, and a joint statement of purpose. They would be otherwise independent. They should also work in six main areas: local government, national planning, social services including family and child care, the provincial media, translations (particularly of French works into English), and regional cultural activities.

Wahl promptly secured funding pledges from three former US ambassadors to France and recruited a steering committee for the American branch of their organization, which would be called the French-American Foundation. Lowenstein, meanwhile, returned to Paris at the end of the month to brief André Gadaud, a member of Giscard's staff whom he had met years before at the French consulate in New York. Gadaud reported that at this point Giscard's reaction to the project was "a blinking green light."

In 1976, the French-American Foundation was ready to launch on both sides of the Atlantic, with each branch having raised $75,000 in start-up funding, organized a steering committee, and appointed executive leadership. In New York, Wahl agreed to serve as founding president; in France, Philippe Bertin-Mourot, a former executive with Avon and Reader's Digest, was appointed executive director. Douglas Dillon, former Secretary of the Treasury and Ambassador to France, agreed to become chairman in New York. The foundation's early programs tracked closely the priorities that the steering committee of the French foundation identified in February 1976. The first was a conference for French and American journalists, which aimed to influence images of the two countries in the mass media. It was held on May 15, 1976, at the School for Advanced International Studies of Johns Hopkins University and it brought together leading journalists from 14 major newspapers, magazines, and other media including the *New York Times*, *The Washington Post*, *Le Monde*, *Le Figaro*, the *Los Angeles Times* and French radio and television.

French president Giscard formally announced the formation of the two French-American Foundations three days later at a dinner for President Ford and Secretary Kissinger at the French embassy in Washington. Lowenstein and Wahl had drafted the French president's remarks, and Lowenstein sent Kissinger a memo briefing him on the new foundation and Giscard's remarks. Kissinger's office returned the memo with a note saying "HAK may have seen." Only years later, at a French-American Foundation gala in New York, would Lowenstein discover that Kissinger had not seen the memo. "You put one over on me, Lowenstein!" Kissinger said when Lowenstein greeted him.[277]

The Embassy dinner took place on May 18, 1976. "Under the guidance of well-known figures," Giscard observed in his toast, the two foundations "will work together closely to further exchanges and dialogue between our two countries. Now, one of the objectives of my visit to which I am most attached will have been achieved. I know, Mr. President, that it meets your wishes too; that is, that France and the United States should know each other better in order to understand each other better." That was as propitious a beginning as any for an enterprise devoted to reconciling two old friends, and it was a sound foundation for the future.

Luxembourg

After Jimmy Carter defeated Gerald Ford in the 1976 general election, Lowenstein became the Bureau of European Affairs representative to the transition team, working with incoming Secretary of State Cyrus Vance. In place of the *realpolitik* of the last eight years, Carter would make human rights, arms control, economic development, and negotiated compromise the pillars of American foreign policy. The contrast on the issue of Eurocommunism was immediately apparent to Lowenstein. Kissinger had worried that the growing electoral strength of the Italian Communist party, together with the end of authoritarian regimes in Portugal and Spain, could present a dangerous degree of Communist influence over some Western European governments. Carter took a different view. Just days into the new administration, with Hartman away, Lowenstein was asked to attend an Oval Office meeting with the President, his National Security Advisor Zbigniew Brzezinski, and Frank Carlucci, the deputy director of the CIA. Pressed on the US strategy for upcoming Italian elections, Carter forswore more active intervention, even as his administration went on to speak out forcefully against any compromise that would see the Communists gain a share of power.[278]

Lowenstein also represented the Bureau of European Affairs before the Presidential Advisory Committee on Ambassadorial Appointments. Known as the Askew Board, after its chairman, former Florida governor Reubin Askew, the board attempted to fulfill a Carter campaign promise that all diplomatic appointments be made on merit, not as a reward for political contributions. Though Carter would manage to increase the ratio of Foreign Service appointees to noncareer appointees from 2 to 1 to 3 to 1 by 1979, it was not an easy policy to implement, as Lowenstein would learn.[279]

Lowenstein knew that an ambassadorial post was widely seen as a possible next step for a principal deputy assistant secretary. He had it on good information that he was at the top of the career list for Sweden, and he looked forward to returning to the country where he had spent a memorable summer as a young man some 30 years earlier and to which had returned often since. Then, sometime in late April, the Director General of the Foreign Service called him with bad news and good news. The bad news? He was not going to Sweden. Carter, despite his commitment to increase the number of career appointees in the ambassadorial ranks, had promised the ambassadorship there to an old supporter, Rodney Kennedy Minott. The good news? He was going to Luxembourg.[280] By coincidence, Richard Moose, who had returned to the State Department as Deputy Under Secretary of State for Management, presided at the swearing in ceremony for his new post.

Not long after the appointment was announced, Lowenstein ran into Kissinger on the street in Washington. "So I hear you're going to Luxembourg as ambassador," said Kissinger. "Yes, I am," Lowenstein replied. "Well, given the performance of many of your predecessors," Kissinger replied, "there's no way even you could screw up that job."[281]

Kissinger was alluding to a long tradition in the State Department of sending noncareer ambassadors to

Luxembourg, a small, wealthy, multilingual country in the heart of Europe. Since 1945, US ambassadors there had been chosen less for their diplomatic skills than for their political connections. Harry Truman had sent Perle Mesta, Washington's "Hostess with the Mostest." Dwight D. Eisenhower had named Texas millionaire Wiley Buchanan. Nixon had made two appointments: Kingdon Gould, a parking magnate and GOP contributor; and Ruth Lewis Farkas, a serious figure—she had a doctorate in education—whose appointment caused an uproar when it was disclosed that her husband, George, had contributed $300,000 to Nixon's re-election campaign.[282] The most recent ambassador had been Rosemary Ginn, a St. Louis publisher and former chair of the Republican National Committee in Missouri. Eager to have a professional diplomat, not a political crony, as US ambassador, the Luxembourg prime minister, Gaston Thorn, had sent his ambassador to the State Department with an *aide-memoire* stating this desire. Lowenstein himself, in Hartman's absence, had received the paper. Thorn, whose handling of a delicate vote on Zionism during his term as president of the United Nations General Assembly had earned him goodwill in Washington, finally got his wish.[283]

Indeed, there could have few more qualified appointees for the US ambassadorship to Luxembourg than Lowenstein. He was a fluent French speaker with extensive connections in the White House and the State Department and he had a ready command of the issues facing the two countries, particularly those related to such multinational institutions as NATO, the OECD, and the European Community. Guy de Muyser, the Marshal of the Court of the Grand Duke, Luxembourg's constitutional monarch, saw in Lowenstein a "quiet assurance. He didn't want to produce fireworks, but he didn't need to." It didn't take long for Lowenstein to make his mark. "He took the place by storm," said Lowenstein's first deputy chief of mission, James D. Phillips. "He didn't need me or anybody else at the Embassy. He could have done the job entirely on his own."

Sometimes it felt as though he might have to do just that. A small embassy, the US mission in Luxembourg had fewer than two dozen staff, of which the largest contingent was the US Marine guard. There was a deputy chief of mission who managed day-to-day operations, an economic officer, a consular officer, an administrative officer, a part-time Defense attaché who was resident in Brussels, two communicators, the marine guards, and several local employees. Lowenstein did most of the political reporting himself.[284]

At the same time, the US ambassador was automatically well regarded because of America's role in World War II. General George S. Patton and his Third Infantry Division had helped liberate the country from German occupation in December 1944. Patton himself was buried in Luxembourg along with more than 5,000 other American soldiers. Since the 1950s, the town of Ettelbruck in central Luxembourg had hosted an annual Remembrance Day, or Patton Day, to show its gratitude. Thirty years later, the United States remained a guarantor of Luxembourg's security through NATO. American banks and industrial firms had also become a major source of direct foreign investment in Luxembourg—$375 million by 1978—which came as the country was on the cusp of changing its economy from steel production to financial services and communications.[285] Many Luxembourg politicians, moreover, had been educated in the United States: the Foreign Minister Colette Flesch at Wellesley and Fletcher; her deputy Paul Helminger at Stanford; the minister of energy Josy Barthel at Harvard; and the minister of agriculture and public works Jean Hamilius at Cornell. In short, Luxembourgers, all 384,000 of them, were distinctly pro-American, and this was reflected in dealings between the Foreign Ministry and the US embassy. As James D. Phillips's successor Charles Higginson said of his main contact at the Luxembourg foreign ministry: "I think he knew that I knew his instructions, which I never saw in writing, but I'm quite sure were 'Never say No to the Americans. Divert them, but never, ever say No to them.'"[286]

Lowenstein, therefore, could steer clear of issues that caused tensions in other Western European capitals, including the American proposal to deploy neutron bombs and differences over relations with Iran after militants stormed the US embassy in Tehran. The one exception was the rise of domestic terrorist groups—Baader Meinhof Group in West Germany, the Red Brigades in Italy, and *Euzkadi ta Azkatasuna* (ETA) in Spain—that forced the US, Luxembourg, and other European countries to work together to combat terrorism on European soil. Where issues did arise, Lowenstein had the added benefit of a close friendship with the Luxembourg prime minister, Thorn. That friendship grew closer still after Lowenstein, recently divorced from Dora after 22 years, began seeing a Frenchwoman, Anne Cornely de la Selle, whom he would later marry. Anne befriended Thorn's wife, Liliane, and the two couples began to socialize regularly.[287]

Because the friendly US-Luxembourg relationship needed relatively little of his attention, Lowenstein focused on multinational issues. When NATO members disagreed over who would register AWACS (airborne warning and control system) planes, the US embassy persuaded Luxembourgers to register them.[288] The Americans also negotiated an agreement with ARBED, the big Luxembourg steel maker, to build a storage facility for American M-60 tanks and other military equipment—Luxembourg's first foreign military installation. The idea was to pre-position equipment that was close to the front line but still distant enough that it would not be overrun in a first attack by Warsaw Pact forces. By the time the facility was built, Luxembourg had more tanks per capita than any country in the world.[289]

The small country of Luxembourg turned out to have an outsized role in European affairs that made it an excellent source of intelligence on multinational issues. The European Council, comprising heads of European Community members states, rotated their summit meetings through Luxembourg and the other member states, while the European Parliament in those days divided its time between Luxembourg City and

Strasbourg, France. The European Investment Bank, the lending arm of the European Community, was headquartered in Luxembourg, as was the European Court of Justice. Lowenstein received some of the best information on European matters from Thorn, who had close ties with the heads of Europe's two largest powers, Giscard d'Estaing of France and Helmut Schmidt of Germany. "He would see Schmidt on Monday, Giscard on Tuesday, and we would have dinner on Wednesday," Lowenstein said. [290]

Lowenstein, like other members of the diplomatic corps in Luxembourg, had limited contact with the royal family apart from the occasional receptions and protocolary events. One exception involved Joan Dillon, the wife of the Grand Duke's younger brother, Prince Charles. Princess Joan was the daughter of Douglas Dillon, the former US Ambassador to France and Secretary of the Treasury. A few months after Lowenstein became ambassador, Prince Charles died. Lowenstein made certain that Princess Joan knew she could count on the US embassy to help with whatever she needed. His friendship with Joan continued long after she married a French aristocrat, Philippe de Noailles, Duc de Mouchy, in 1978. Lowenstein often visited the couple in the following years at their country house.

The ambassadorship, of course, came with social duties as well. Without a spouse to assist in organizing the many dinners and other events on the embassy calendar, Lowenstein was fortunate to have capable assistants like Wanda Kennicott, an American, Myriam Norris-Zigrand, a Luxembourger, as well as Genevra Higginson, the wife of his deputy chief of mission. Together, they managed to work with a small entertainment allowance—small because Lowenstein's predecessors had deep pockets.[291]

The embassy also had its share of houseguests. The highest-ranking US official to visit during Lowenstein's time was Warren Burger, the Chief Justice of the US Supreme Court, who had traveled to Luxembourg to meet his counterparts on the European Court of Justice. Burger regaled embassy staff with a documentary film of major constitutional law cases and then talked past two in the morning. [292] With weekend staff in short supply, Deputy Chief of Mission Higginson was forced to run the film projector. There were US Congressional delegations too along with journalists who descended on Luxembourg for European Council meetings.[293] The most challenging visitors came in Lowenstein's second summer, when he had almost a hundred house guests between the ages of 13 and 19—nieces, nephews, and friends of his children, Laurinda and Price. With ambassadors responsible for the food and wine bills of their personal guests, Lowenstein had to worry that this steady stream of guests would break the bank. Eventually he put a lock on the beer and wine and established four inexpensive set menus. This did not go over well with two student houseguests, whom he heard say when coming down for dinner one night, "Not *choucroute garnie* again!"[294]

In October 1979, Margaret Thatcher came to Luxembourg to give the annual Winston Churchill Memorial Lecture. Before an audience of foreign ambassadors from east and west, the new British prime minister talked of the meaning and obligations of liberty and how they had shaped her vision of Europe and the European Community. Her speech, however, was also a blistering assault on Communism. The Soviet and Eastern European diplomats in attendance all walked out. "That's the kind of speech that I don't think an American politician would have made in that setting," Lowenstein told Thatcher later at a British embassy dinner in her honor. "Well, Al Haig would have made that speech," she said. When Lowenstein pointed out that Haig was not an American politician," Thatcher replied: "Ah, yes, but he will be." She was correct, of course. Haig went on to serve as US Secretary of State for two years under President Ronald Reagan.

The embassy dinner was hosted by the British ambassador Patrick Wright. He became head of the diplomatic service while Margaret Thatcher was still Prime Minister, and he was eventually elevated to the House of Lords as Lord Wright of

Richmond. Lowenstein and Wright became close, lifelong friends. One day, when Lowenstein was with Wright in the House of Lords, they came upon Thatcher in a corridor. At that point, Thatcher was beginning to lose her memory. Wright stopped her and introduced Lowenstein, saying, "You met him in Luxembourg." Ever polite, Thatcher said, "Of course."

In addition to attending embassy functions and other official diplomatic functions, Lowenstein made the rounds of the many private dinner parties given by Luxembourg politicians and by bankers, industrialists, and foreign diplomats.[295] Beneath this upper stratum, life in Luxembourg slowed considerably. Despite having the second-highest per capita income in Europe, the country was still fairly provincial, with nothing like the cultural life that exists today. As Phillips told Higginson when Higginson became DCM: "If you get bored, you can always go down to the railroad station and watch the trains go in and out."[296]

Lowenstein, though, never let himself get bored. No matter what else he had on his agenda, he always made time for a game of tennis or squash, which connected him to members of the government and Luxembourg society. Though he was in his early 50s, he continued to perform at a high level on the tennis court, playing—and beating—his assistant's boyfriends, all 25 years his junior.[297] He also traveled for pleasure. He visited the Swiss Alpine town Klosters for skiing and Great Britain to see friends. Lowenstein also made regular visits to Paris, where the US ambassador, his longtime friend and mentor Arthur Hartman, had offered him a guest room at the Embassy residence when available.

More than most US ambassadors to Luxembourg, Lowenstein interwove the social and diplomatic aspects of the job. Three former Luxembourg officials—Colette Flesch, Paul Helminger, and Guy de Muyser—would all use the same word to describe Lowenstein's approach: integrated.[298] "He made lots of friends in diplomatic [and] government circles, but also in the general public," recalled Helminger. "He…formed some really good and long-lasting friendships with people who had nothing to do with politics or diplomacy, but that were simply lively members of Luxembourg society."

In this spirit, Lowenstein also saw his ambassadorship as a way to engage a wide community of Americans and Luxembourgers in dialogue. To advance public diplomacy, he got approval for a local United States Information Agency post, staffed first by his former assistant, Myriam Norris-Zygrand, and later by a Luxembourg journalist, Yoland Wilvers.[299] He initiated an annual Luxembourg-American senior tennis tournament called the Lux-Am Plate, persuading senior tournament players in the 45-plus age bracket who were passing through Europe to stop in Luxembourg and compete against a team of Luxembourgers.[300] Lowenstein also founded a foreign policy think tank, the Société Luxembourgeoise des Affaires Internationales (known in Luxembourg by its initials, SLI) and recruited Marcel Mart, a Luxembourg politician and former cabinet minister, to head it. It was the Luxembourg equivalent of the Council on Foreign Relations and it became a forum for Luxembourg's increasingly vital role as a liaison between France and Germany. To fund SLI, Lowenstein signed up a wealthy German-American, Henry J. Leir, who was a donor to various American charities in Europe.[301] SLI survived for many years after Lowenstein left Luxembourg.

In Lowenstein's third year as ambassador, he learned that a friend of Senator George McGovern's was interested in the post. But with just one more year left in Carter's first term, Thorn asked the US Secretary of State, Cyrus Vance, to keep Lowenstein as ambassador, which he agreed to do.[302]

Thorn's intervention with Vance reflected what Lowenstein meant to US-Luxembourg relations. He promoted American interests in Luxembourg as well as Luxembourg interests in America. He ran the embassy as a serious and efficient enterprise. He forged close relationships with senior members of the Luxembourg government and attracted American business investment at a time when Luxembourg was moving to diversify its economy. He also helped raise Luxembourg's profile inside the US State Department, which Luxembourgers appreciated. Recalled De Muyser: "We sometimes felt that in Jim, we had a direct advocate in Washington for the interest of Luxembourg."[303]

After Ronald Reagan defeated Carter in November 1980, Lowenstein knew it would soon be time to leave. He learned that his replacement would be John E. Dolibois, a Luxembourger by birth who had interrogated Nazi war criminals at the Nuremberg trials before going on to become the vice president of the University of Miami in Ohio. Career appointees like Lowenstein normally stayed on until they were replaced. With Dolibois not scheduled to arrive until the fall, Lowenstein agreed to remain through the summer. He used his time to plan the transition to the new ambassador, and he made plans to marry his fiancée, Anne, in Luxembourg on the Fourth of July. The day before his wedding, however, as he looked out of the embassy residence at his soon-to-be in-laws arriving by car, he was handed a cable instructing him to leave Luxembourg in 72 hours.

Furious, Lowenstein protested to his friend Lawrence Eagleburger, then Assistant Secretary for European Affairs. He was determined not to leave the embassy without first paying farewell calls to the Grand Duke and members of the Luxembourg government. Such courtesies were considered customary for a departing diplomat—not least for Lowenstein, who was the senior member of the diplomatic corps in Luxembourg. Eagleburger was able to obtain a one-week delay. In that time, Lowenstein called on as many government ministers as he could find. The Grand Duke, who was away on holiday, returned for a day in order to receive Lowenstein, while Foreign Minister Colette Flesch and the French ambassador each gave a small dinner in his honor.[304] Just before leaving, Lowenstein was decorated with the Grand Croix de la Ordre de la Couronne de chêne (Grand Cross of the Order of the Oak Crown), the highest grade of this Luxembourg order.

Lowenstein attributed the fiasco of his departure to Reagan's new Secretary of State, Alexander Haig. The chief of staff in Nixon's White House, Haig could had not liked

Richard Moose since the days when Haig first arrived from the Pentagon and Moose was staff secretary of the National Security Council. In addition, the Lowenstein/Moose reports had made life difficult for the Nixon administration and made Lowenstein another target of Haig's ire.[305] Lowenstein returned to Washington in late July, determined to protest his shabby treatment regarding his departure from Luxembourg. But in a State Department now led by Haig, no one would see him. Lowenstein remained in the Foreign Service for another year, taking on a variety of responsibilities in the Bureau of European Affairs. On his final day, there was no fanfare. He went to the Director General's outer office, collected the ambassadorial flag issued to him as Luxembourg chief of mission, and left. "As so often happens in the Foreign Service," he later reflected, "departure is the low point of one's experience."[306] In Lowenstein's case, at least, it was the only low point. "I was very lucky in the Foreign Service because I never had a boring job. I know they are there, but I never had one."[307]

Epilogue: Later Years

Lowenstein's retirement has lasted longer than his 32 years in government service. It has been nearly as active.

IRC

In 1983, a year after leaving the State Department, Lowenstein cofounded a small consulting firm called the International Relations Consultants Group (IRC). His fellow partners were three former colleagues: William vanden Heuvel, Ambassador to the European Headquarters of the UN in Geneva, Michael Sterner, Ambassador to the United Arab Emirates, and Donald McHenry, US Permanent Representative to the UN in New York. Vanden Heuvel, a well-connected Manhattan lawyer, was a generalist, while the others worked mainly for clients in their geographic areas of expertise: Sterner in the Middle East, McHenry in Africa, and Lowenstein in Europe. They shared overhead but otherwise operated independently. Their overall purpose was to continue doing interesting work.[308]

Lowenstein signed up two major clients, which he served in various capacities over the next 15 years. One was Marsh & McLennan, the holding company for the insurance brokerage Marsh and the risk management and reinsurance specialist Guy Carpenter. Lowenstein worked closely with Brandon W.

Sweitzer, the chief financial officer and later president of Marsh and the president and CEO of Guy Carpenter. He advised Sweitzer and his leadership teams on political risk, both in Europe and in apartheid-era South Africa. He accompanied Sweitzer on trips abroad, including trips to Turkey when Marsh was negotiating the purchase of an insurance company there. He took the Marsh board of directors to Budapest and Prague after the 1989 revolutions, as the company was planning its entry into Eastern Europe, and he later advised them on regulations involving the European Union. Lowenstein also represented Marsh and Guy Carpenter at insurance conferences throughout Europe.[309]

Lowenstein's other major client was David H. Swanson—first at Continental Grain, then the world's largest commodity trading concern, where Swanson headed the small but fast-growing financial services division, and then at Central Soya, another agribusiness company, where Swanson was president and CEO.

In 1999, Continental spun off its commodity trading business and reorganized itself as a holding company, ContiGroup Companies. In 2002, Central Soya was acquired by agribusiness giant Bunge.

Lowenstein advised David Swanson and his successor David Banks at Continental as they negotiated countertrade agreements for the exchange of goods and services rather than hard currency throughout Eastern Europe.

Lowenstein's contribution to these deals was his grasp of the human side of business. For example, in a Romanian countertrade deal, Romaero, a Romanian aircraft maker, was manufacturing a version of the BAC1-11 passenger airliner under license by the British government, but the British engineers on the project had never been paid. Furious, Margaret Thatcher got Continental Grain involved to see if they could help Romania settle their debt through the purchase of British goods, as Romania was short on hard currency. After negotiations had dragged on for weeks, Lowenstein said to Continental's lead negotiator. "You don't understand what this negotiation is about. This negotiation is about the fact that the Romanian minister of aviation wants to be invited to the Farnborough air show with his girlfriend, all expenses paid. Why don't you make an offer and see what happens?"

The 1980s was a good time to launch a business like IRC. In the early days of globalization, American multinationals were hungry for the sorts of insights that former Foreign Service officers had to offer, insights that few others had at the time. As the need for such services grew, however, many companies began to build this expertise in-house, or they farmed out the work to their law firms, which had moved aggressively into this area.

Lowenstein left IRC in 1991, though he continued as a consultant to Sweitzer and Swanson until the late 1990s. He worked on his own for a couple of years before he and his friend Arthur Hartman teamed up and worked loosely under the umbrella of the newly-formed APCO Associates, then part of the law firm of Arnold and Porter. APCO Associates left Arnold and Porter in 1991 and is now APCO Worldwide. His IRC partners stayed on at IRC for a few years before winding it down, McHenry and vanden Heuvel to devote their time to an investment firm where each had a stake, and Sterner to do more writing and speechmaking unencumbered by potential conflicts of interest.[310]

Writing and Speaking

Lowenstein also managed to do some writing and speaking of his own. In the early 1980s, his op-eds in the *New York Times* and the *International Herald Tribune* dealt with US-European relations. In the 1990s, his op-eds in *The Washington Post* and the *International Herald Tribune* focused on the violent breakup of the former Yugoslavia. He also lectured on US foreign policy in Belgrade, Bonn, Sofia, Stockholm, and Athens.

Election Observer Missions

The geographic expertise Lowenstein had gained early in his State Department career led to invitations to serve as an election observer. The first came from the government of Sri Lanka. In March 1993, he spent a week in Bandarawela, Sri Lanka, a town in the hill country, where he observed preparations for the provincial council elections in May. Two weeks later, a suicide bomber took the life of Sri Lanka's president, Ranasinghe Premadasa, who belonged to the ruling United National Party (UNP), which had been in power for 17 years. Responsibility was claimed by a member of the militant rebel group Tamil Tigers. It was against this backdrop of violence that Lowenstein returned to Sri Lanka in August 1994 for the parliamentary elections. Security on election day was tight, and Lowenstein and other international observers affirmed that voting was free and fair. In the end, the People's Alliance, a group of opposition parties, won enough support to form a government, marking a decisive break with the UNP.

Lowenstein also served as an election observer in Bosnia and Herzegovina following the Dayton Agreement of 1995. In 1996 and 1997, as a senior adviser to Ambassador Robert Frowick, head of the Organization for Security and Co-operation in Europe (OSCE) mission that had been charged with implementing the non-military aspects of the Dayton Agreement, he oversaw the integrity of a series of parliamentary and presidential polls in Bosnia and Herzegovina and in Republika Srpska, which was a majority Serbian territory of Bosnia. OSCE paid his expenses, but he volunteered his time and he returned every three months for two or three weeks over the two-year period.

The mission returned Lowenstein to Sarajevo, where he had served as a food aid observer with the US Special Mission to Yugoslavia in 1950 and 1951. In some respects, the city looked better than it did then, thanks to decades of economic development. Still, the nearly four-year siege of Sarajevo by Bosnian Serbs had clearly taken its toll on the city and its people. Many Bosnian Serbs expressed no remorse for that onslaught, as Lowenstein saw first-hand. At one point, he was asked to go to Pale, the de facto capital of Republika Srpska, to collect Nikola Koljević, the vice president of Republika Srpska, and bring him to Sarajevo for a ceremony. A respected academic at the University of Sarajevo in the 1970s and 1980s and one of the foremost Shakespearean scholars in Yugoslavia, Koljević was an urbane, jovial figure who had taught at numerous American universities. After the death of his son in a mountain climbing accident, he took solace in his Serbian cultural heritage, eventually becoming a hardened Serbian nationalist and participating in the siege of Sarajevo. Lowenstein and Koljević were accompanied by Italian *Carabinieri* riding in armored vehicles, as Koljević was terrified that he would be assassinated if he returned. As they approached Sarajevo, Lowenstein asked him how it felt to return to the city where he had lived for so many years and which was now ruined by war. Koljević was unapologetic. "I should have stayed in America," was all he could find to say. It was not long after this encounter that Koljević, stripped of political power, took his own life.[311]

Toward the end of his missions to Bosnia, Lowenstein had occasion to return to Belgrade under unusual circumstances. One afternoon in November 1997, when he was in Brčko, a disputed territory in northern Bosnia, he received a telephone call from Ambassador Frowick telling him that if he could make it to the Sarajevo airport by 8 am the following morning, he could accompany Frowick on his farewell call on Slobodan Milošević, the notorious President of Yugoslavia and former president of Serbia. Lowenstein managed to find someone with a jeep to drive him over the mountains that night. The next day, Ambassador Frowick and Lowenstein met with Milošević at the White Palace, where Tito had once received official visitors. For Lowenstein, the meeting began in a surreal fashion: Milošević was seated where Tito had sat, Frowick was seated where US ambassadors had been seated when calling on Tito, and Lowenstein was seated in the very spot where he taken notes during a meeting between Tito and the US ambassador. At one point in the conversation, Milošević turned to Lowenstein and said, "So, you've been here before. What do you think?" Lowenstein responded, "I never thought I'd see the day when Serbia was one of the poorest countries in Europe."

In 2001, Milošević would be extradited to the UN International Criminal Tribunal for the Former Yugoslavia at The Hague to stand trial for genocide. He died in prison of natural causes in 2006.

Serving on Boards

Much of Lowenstein's professional life since the mid-1990s has been taken up with serving on boards of directors, both private and nonprofit. Ties to Sweitzer and Swanson led him to become a director of several large offshore investment funds, including Emerging Eastern Europe Fund Ltd., the first fund to focus on assets in the former Warsaw Pact nations. Launched weeks after the 1989 revolutions and operated by Continental Grain's trading arm, the fund set out to finance projects that could earn export income. That was the intention behind the fund's investment in a cornflakes factory in western Poland, which exported most of its production to West Germany because most Poles could not afford cornflakes for breakfast. But with the success of economic liberalization there, the plant's entire output would soon end up going to the Polish domestic market.[312]

Privatization did not go as smoothly everywhere. For example, Lowenstein became chairman of the Ukraine Fund Ltd., a $90 million closed-end mutual fund established in 1997 by Ladenburg Thalmann, a New York investment firm, and French bank Société Générale. The fund aimed to scoop up shares of undervalued metallurgical, chemical, and industrial companies and realize profits as great as those earned by money managers in post-Soviet Russia. Ukraine, however, turned out to be a case study in the challenges of building a market economy almost from scratch. It was a country "where you had an agreement until you didn't have an agreement," said Lowenstein. At one point, unhappy investors wanted to wind up the fund and sell the assets, but the principal of the fund, John D. Chapman, elected instead to start afresh. He removed the entire board except for Lowenstein, whose knowledge of Eastern Europe and ties to US government officials in Washington and the US embassy in Kiev would prove immensely valuable. Lowenstein contributed a shrewd intelligence and a good instinct for the human element in business, traits that helped the boards he served on negotiate successfully.[313]

In addition to serving on boards, Lowenstein has served as a trustee of several nonprofits, perhaps none more important to him than two with French connections. One was the American Library in Paris, which was founded in 1920 with books and periodicals that had been donated to American soldiers and sailors during World War I. The Library had evolved into an intellectual refuge for the American expatriate community in Paris and a center for English-language literature, learning, and culture in France. First as a trustee and since 2009 as chair of the Advisory Council, Lowenstein has counseled the library's executive staff on outreach and fundraising. The other nonprofit was the French-American Foundation (FAF).

The French-American Foundation

Lowenstein continues to work with the French-American Foundation, which he cofounded in 1976 with Professor Nicholas Wahl, then at Princeton University and later Director of the Institute of French Studies at NYU. In 1988, Wahl had married Boris Johnson's mother Charlotte. That event introduced a future Prime Minister to the French American Foundation. In 2015, when Johnson was still mayor of London, Lowenstein drafted a letter for the chairman of the French foundation inviting Johnson to be a guest of honor at the following year's gala and receive an award honoring his father-in-law Wahl, who had died in 1996. Johnson responded with warm words for Wahl and the foundation and explained that he was about to leave the mayoralty and would be busy running for parliament. He said, however, that he hoped to attend the following year. By that time he was Foreign Secretary and couldn't attend then either. But the possibility exists that he will one day attend. Lowenstein is no longer on the board of the New York or Paris foundations, but is now honorary vice chairman of both and helps promote the foundation's programs.

One of the foundation's most imaginative programs was the "French Teachers of English Study Tour." Launched in the FAF's maiden year, it brought instructors from French secondary schools to the United States to learn about federal, state, and municipal government, the judicial system, and industry, agriculture, media, and religion. The perspective they gained, both through formal study and from the families that hosted them in small cities like Baltimore, Maryland; Lincoln, Nebraska; and Freeport, Illinois, made it less likely they would express anti-American sentiments when they returned home. A similar program in the 1980s sent US congressmen and congresswomen to live for a time with their French counterparts, helping to soften attitudes toward the French on Capitol Hill. In the early 1990s, the Clinton administration's push for healthcare reform spurred the launch of the FAF's "A Welcome for Every Child" program, which over the next 14 years gathered study teams from both countries to examine the benefits of French early education and maternal and child healthcare systems. The goal, explained FAF trustee Arthur Hartman, was "to bring to America something the French really do right, which is early education….They start before the child is born and give mothers special treatment. It is a much better system in terms of a social approach to a healthy young population." Another small program conceived by Elizabeth Rohatyn, the wife of American financier and then US ambassador Felix Rohaytn, brought together curators from small museums on both sides of the Atlantic. In addition,

FAF fellowships in the late 1990s and early 2000s made it possible for French and American journalists to work with and learn from each other. And today's FAF working group on cybersecurity had its roots in an early 2000s conference, where representatives of the US military, which ended compulsory military service in 1973, shared their perspectives on the transition to a professional army with their French counterparts, who eliminated conscription in 2001.[314]

Perhaps the activity that best embodies this emphasis on nurturing mutual understanding through shared experiences is the FAF's signature program, Young Leaders, the brainchild of Ezra Suleiman, a professor of politics at Princeton. Every year the FAF selects 10 French and 10 Americans between the ages of 30 and 40 for the two-year program. Participants spend a long weekend together in either France or the United States in the first year, and a long weekend in the other country in the second year. During those weekends they discuss issues of common concern. The Young Leaders program suffered an interruption in 1989 when it was discontinued. Lowenstein and Hartman finally intervened in 1993, threatening to resign from the FAF board if the program were not revived. Young Leaders resumed the following year and has continued without interruption ever since.

While Suleiman had made the selections himself in the first few years, the Young Leaders were subsequently selected by a jury of former participants in the program. These participants now come from a wide range of fields—a legacy of the program's founding circumstances. It was established in March 1981, when President Ronald Reagan had become wary of the socialist François Mitterand, who would soon be leading France. To foster dialogue between France and America, the Young Leaders program was determined to seek out voices not just from traditional diplomatic, government, and military channels but also from the business, media, and nonprofit sectors.[315] Young Leaders is shaped by another organizing principle: that elites, by virtue of their intellect and achievements, play a more important role than might be expected from those of their age in shaping relationships between nations. This principle has remained central to Young Leaders.

Supported by Francophile and philanthropist Anne Cox Chambers until her death in 2020, the Young Leaders program has an impressive list of alumni on both sides of the Atlantic, including Secretary of State Anthony Blinken, former US President Bill Clinton, former Secretary of State Hillary Clinton, Los Angeles Mayor Eric Garcetti, retired General Wesley Clark, Pulitzer Prize writer Isobel Wilkerson, former Governor of Louisiana Bobby Jindal, Dean of the Columbia School of Journalism Steve Coll, former Chairman and CEO of AXA Henri de Castries, former Chairman of Merrill Lynch John Thain, former World Bank president Robert Zoellick, European Space Agency French astronaut Thomas Pesquet, mathematician and French politician Cédric Villani, former French prime ministers Alain Marie Juppé and Édouard Philippe, former French president François Hollande, and current French president Emmanuel Macron.

"We've been very good at selecting people," noted Vivien de Gunzburg, a member of the 2012 class of Young Leaders. "Most of them became great successes and very well-known in their fields. The beauty is that they know how the other side of the Atlantic thinks, and they remain in touch."[316]

In recent years, the FAF has had to navigate an evolving French-American relationship. The economic and political muscle of the European Union has amplified France's influence on the world stage, just as Jean Monnet envisioned, but it has sometimes led American policymakers to prioritize issues that involve Europe as a whole. There is also a demographic problem because a generation of wealthy, well-connected Francophiles in the United States is dying out with no comparable generation to replace it.[317] Neither challenge is entirely new. France has always had significant influence in European affairs, and the close ties between French and American leaders forged during the postwar era were beginning to wane when Lowenstein and Wahl established the FAF. That was the prime reason that Lowenstein and Wahl established the FAF in the first place.

Where the FAF has been most successful has been in the service of its founding mission, which is to strengthen the French-American relationship in political and economic areas. Lowenstein, as the organization's *éminence grise*, encourages the FAF to remain true to this mission. Time and again, he has sought to move the organization forward and to imagine the next generation of ideas and activities that will help the FAF fulfill its mission. "He's not telling you about the stories from 50 years ago," explained Jean-Luc Allavena, the former chair of the French-American Foundation in France. "He's using [that experience] for what it's worth in the future, and that's fantastic."[318] It was for his contributions to the FAF and to the French-American relationship as a whole, that Lowenstein was twice decorated with the *Légion d'Honneur*, the highest French order of merit: first in 1990 as a *chevalier* (knight) and then in 2005 as an *officier*.

Octogenarians Without Borders

Age, meanwhile, has done little to diminish Lowenstein's physical energy and intellectual vitality, even as a single man (Lowenstein and his second wife, Anne, divorced in 2000 after 19 years of marriage). Through organizations such as the Council on Foreign Relations, the International Institute for Strategic Studies in London, and the Institut Français des Relations Internationales in Paris, he has maintained a keen interest in foreign affairs. As journalist and broadcaster Marvin Kalb said, "He continued to live in that world [of diplomacy and foreign affairs] and be accepted in that world [long after he left the State Department].... To this day, he cares about issues that affect this country and what can be done to help this country."[319] Eager to remain active, Lowenstein launched a business venture in 2010 with John W. Barnum, a Yale classmate, friend from Paris days, former corporate lawyer, and former US deputy secretary of transportation. They gave their venture the somewhat tongue-in-cheek name "Octogenarians without Borders" with the idea of offering free consulting services. However, things did not work out as planned. "John had several clients who were getting free legal advice. I had none," said Lowenstein.

Tennis

Although he no longer takes an annual ski trip to Klosters, Switzerland, having given up skiing at age 83, Lowenstein had continued to play tennis until three years ago. Ranked number 56 nationally in the United States Tennis Association 80 and over men's singles in 2009, he competed in senior tournaments as recently as 2017, when he played in the 90 and over National Clay Court Singles Championships. There were just nine entrants. Lowenstein lost in the first round to William (Bill) Weathers, a longtime Southern Tennis Hall of Fame honoree. The stands were filled with players in their eighties who got a rare glimpse of what tennis in their nineties might be like if they were lucky. In previous years, he had played in a number of International Club (IC) tournaments in Europe, including the Potter Cup, named after his longtime friend, John Potter.

Travels

In all this time, Lowenstein has never ceased traveling the world, either for professional reasons or for pleasure. Since he retired from the Foreign Service in 1982, he has been to India, Sri Lanka, Vietnam, Laos, Thailand, Burma, Romania, Cyprus, Spain, Ukraine, Russia, Greece, Poland, Hungary, South Korea, Peru, Croatia, Jordan, Lebanon, Iran, Syria, Israel, Palestine, Egypt, Turkey, Bulgaria, Russia, the Czech Republic, Slovakia, Lithuania, Latvia, Estonia, Slovenia, Bosnia, Morocco, Malta, Qatar, the United Arab Emirates, the United Kingdom (including Channel Islands Jersey and Guernsey), Belgium, Luxembourg, Germany, Switzerland, Monaco, Chile, Cuba, Kenya, South Africa, and Namibia.

Some of his travel in the past decade has been on tours with a foreign affairs focus and have included briefings and meetings with government ministers, opposition leaders, local guides, and political experts. Marvin Kalb joked that wherever he went, Lowenstein "was always the guy at a dinner party in the dead of winter with a sunburn, just back from somewhere."[320] He continues to spend four to five months each year at his *pied-à-terre* in Paris's seventh arrondissement, and he spends summers in Northeast Harbor, Maine, often joined by his companion, literary agent Audrey Wolf.

Family

Lowenstein's family has been every bit as important to him as his career and other interests. His daughter, Laurinda, who was born in Washington but spent her early years in Colombo and Belgrade before returning to Washington, is married to a Yale- and Cambridge-educated lawyer, Edward Douglas, and lives in New York City and Seal Harbor, Maine. Their son, Alex, has just graduated from Georgetown University. Lowenstein's son, Price, who was born in Colombo, lives in Bermuda, where he is the founder and head of the political risk insurance firm Sovereign Risk Ltd. and has an apartment in New York. A widower since 2006 when his wife, Carolyn Burgett Lowenstein, died of cancer, he will marry Dr. Laura MacIsaac, an obstetrical surgeon, in August. Price's son, Jake, who finished Pepperdine business school last year, has embarked on a career at Bank of America. His daughter, Haley, lives in Denver, where she is pursuing a graduate degree in social work. To children and grandchildren alike, Lowenstein has been a model of stability and calm and a source of wise counsel.[321] There is no Grant Cottage to bring them all together, as there was in Lowenstein's youth, but there is Maine in the summer, and Lowenstein keeps in close contact with this children and grandchildren throughout the year, as he does with his brother Peter, his sister-in-law, Connie, and the his late brother Hugh's widow, Sandy.

Conclusion

On March 12, 2020, Lowenstein was in London after a week attending a conference and seeing friends. He was due to leave the following day for a week in Budapest and then three weeks in Paris. At 4 am, he was alerted to President Trump's speech imposing an international travel ban to begin two days later in response to the rapidly spreading COVID-19 pandemic. He immediately booked a flight leaving for Washington that afternoon. After 15 months under COVID restrictions, as his 94th birthday approaches, Lowenstein is looking forward to resuming as many of his activities as possible. He has recounted these activities, as well as the story of their heritage, for future generations of the family in the hope that they too will be inspired to involve themselves in the wider world beyond their nation's borders.

Notes

Prologue

1. Harriet Stryker-Rodda, ed., *Price – Goldsmith – Lowenstein and Related Families: 1700-1967*, from the collected notes of Katherine Goldsmith Lowenstein (Privately printed, 1967), p. 1.

2. Stryker-Rodda, ed., *Price – Goldsmith – Lowenstein*, pp. 16ff, 31. "Pioneer Butcher, August Lowenstein, Dies at the Age of 71 Years," *Cincinnati Enquirer,* December 22, 1898, https://www.newspapers.com/clip/6586660/august-lowenstein-dies/.

3. According to the family genealogy, Moss was born in 1824 and died in 1906. However, a local newspaper, *The Central New Jersey Home News* of New Brunswick has his birth and death years as 1823 and 1905, respectively. Stryker-Rodda, ed., *Price – Goldsmith – Lowenstein*, p. 5. "Aged Col. Moss Dies at Metuchen," *The Central New Jersey Home News*, April 21, 1905, p. 1. https://www.newspapers.com/clip/17505801/joseph-lafayette-moss-obituary/

4. JL1 interview,

5. "Gen. Grant's Cottage Sold," *New York Times,* December 4, 1893.

6. Ron Chernow, *Grant* (Penguin Press, 2017), p. 650. "Grant Cottage, Owned by Price Family for Past 50 Years, Will Get Plaque," *The Newark Sunday Call*, July 16, 1939.

7. Stryker-Rodda, ed., *Price – Goldsmith – Lowenstein*, p. 20.

8. JL1 interview. "Francis Wellman: Trial Lawyer," *Trial Guides,* https://www.trialguides.com/blogs/authors/francis-wellman (accessed December 14, 2020). "Melvyn Lowenstein Dies at 79; Was Specialist in

Financial Law," *New York Times*, September 6, 1971. Robert M. Jarvis, "Babe Ruth as Legal Hero," *Florida State University Law Review*, Vol. 22, Issue 4 (Spring 1995), pp. 886-7, note 7, https://core.ac.uk/download/pdf/217315919.pdf.

9   JL1 interview. "J. Paul Carey, Car Renter, Dies," *New York Times*, June 20, 1973, https://www.nytimes.com/1973/06/20/archives/j-paul-carey-74-car-renter-dies-prominent-catholic-laymanserved.html. "Melvyn Lowenstein Dies at 79." Jarvis, "Babe Ruth as Legal Hero," pp. 886-7, note 7. Babe Ruth as told to Bob Considine, *The Babe Ruth Story* (New York: E. P. Dutton & Co., 1948), p. 107.

10 JL1 interview.

11 JL1 interview.

12 JL1 interview. *The Loomis Alumni Bulletin*, n.d.

13 JL1 interview. "W. S. Knickerbocker," *New York Times*, January 17, 1972.

14 JL1 interview.

15 Judith Schiff, "Yale after World War II," *Yale Alumni Magazine*, July-August 2016, https://yalealumnimagazine.com/articles/4312-yale-after-world-war-ii

16 Judith Schiff, "Yale after World War II," *Yale Alumni Magazine*. Brita Belli, "Yale and World War II—reflections from members of the class of '48," *Yale Alumni Magazine,* June 13, 2018, https://news.yale.edu/2018/06/13/yale-and-world-war-ii-reflections-members-class-48.

17 JL1 interview.

18 JL1 interview.

19 JL1 interview.

20 JL1 interview.

Chapter 1

21 Charles L. Mee, Jr., *The Marshall Plan* (New York: Simon & Schuster, 1985), p. 249.

22 Tony Judt, *Postwar: A History of Europe Since 1945* (New York: Penguin, 2005), pp. 82ff.

23 JL1 interview.

24 JL1 interview.

25 Kenneth Weisbrode, *The Atlanticists: A Story of American Diplomacy* (New York: Nortia Press, 2015), p. TK

26 Theodore A. Wilson, *Oral History Interview with Leland Barrows*, January 8, 1971. Harry S. Truman Library and Museum, https://www.trumanlibrary.gov/library/oral-histories/barrowsl

27 Geoffrey Kabaservice, *The Guardians: Kingman Brewster, His Circle, and the Rise of the Liberal Establishment* (New York: Henry Holt and Company, 2014), p. 115. JL1 interview.

28 Antony Beevor and Artemis Cooper, *Paris: After the Liberation, 1945-1949* (New York: Penguin, 1994), p. 355.

29 JL1 interview.

30 Vivien de Gunzburg interview.

31 JL1 interview.

32 Quoted in Greg Behrman, *The Most Noble Adventure: The Marshall Plan and the Time When America Helped Save Europe* (New York: Simon and Schuster, 2007), p. 197.

33 JL1 interview.

34 Judt, *Postwar*, pp. 46, 61.

35 JL1 interview.

36 JL1 interview.

37 JL1 interview.

38 https://www.trumanlibrary.gov/library/personal-papers/everett-h-bellows-papers#bio
    https://history.state.gov/departmenthistory/people/foster-william-chapman

39 "Area Men, ECA Associates Find Yugoslavs Pro-American," undated press clipping. JL1 interview.

40 Lorraine M. Lees, *Keeping Tito Afloat: The United States, Yugoslavia, and the Cold War* (University Park, Pennsylvania: Pennsylvania State University Press, 1997), pp. 53-78

41 Lees, *Keeping Tito Afloat*, pp. 84, 90.

42 Lees, *Keeping Tito Afloat*, p. 92-95.

43 https://jamanetwork.com/journals/jama/article-abstract/261235

44 Charles Stuart Kennedy and John A. Baker, Jr., *Interview with John A. Baker, Jr.*, 1992. Manuscript/Mixed Material, https://www.loc.gov/item/mfdipbib000039//.

45 JL1 Interview. Charles Stuart Kennedy and Leonard Unger, *Interview with Leonard Unger*, 1989. Manuscript/Mixed Material, http://cdn.loc.gov/service/mss/mfdip/2004/2004ung01/2004ung01.pdf.

46 JL1 interview.

47 JL1 interview.

48 Charles Stuart Kennedy and Thomas P. H. Dunlop, *Interview with Thomas P. H. Dunlop*, 1996, Manuscript/Mixed Material, https://www.adst.org/OH%20TOCs/Dunlop,%20Thomas%20PH.toc.pdf.

49 JL1 interview.

50 "Area Men, ECA Associates Find Yugoslavs Pro-American," undated press clipping. Kennedy and Baker, *Interview with John A. Baker, Jr.*

51 JL1 interview.

52 JL1 interview.

53 Kennedy and Baker, *Interview with John A. Baker, Jr.*

54 JL1 interview. https://amblussemburgo.esteri.it/ambasciata_lussemburgo/it/archivio_news

55 JL1 interview.

56 Joseph Lyford, "European Diary: Conversation on a Mountain," n.d. [contemporaneous], unknown publication.

57 Lees, *Keeping Tito Afloat*, p. 97.

58 Kennedy and Baker, *Interview with John A. Baker, Jr.*

59 JLSupp1 interview.

60 Bruce L. R. Smith, *Lincoln Gordon: Architect of Cold War Foreign Policy* (Louisville, Kentucky: University of Kentucky, 2015), pp. 182-187.

61 Ibid.

62 JL1 interview. James G. Lowenstein, "Marshall Plan Days," remarks on the 70th anniversary of the Marshall Plan, US Embassy Marshall Center at the Hotel Talleyrand, Paris, June 1, 2017.

63 Benn Steil, *The Marshall Plan: Dawn of the Cold War* (New York: Simon & Schuster, 2018), pp. 342-343, 345-346.

64 Lees, *Keeping Tito Afloat*, p. 111ff.

65 Judt, *Postwar*, pp. 82ff.

66 Judt, *Postwar*, pp. 155-157.

Chapter 2

67 JL2 interview.

68 JL2 interview.

69 JL1 interview. Kai Bird, *The Chairman: John J. McCloy and the Making of the American Establishment* (New York: Simon & Schuster, 1992), pp.

316-7. "William H. Willis, Jr., Longtime Greenwich Resident," *Greenwich Daily Voice,* May 15, 2014.

70   JL2 interview.
71   https://usscoralsea.net/pics1950s1.php
72   JL2 interview.
73   JL2 interview.
74   JLSupp1 interview.
75   JL2 interview.
76   JL2 interview.
77   Thomas H. Robbins, "The Study of International Law at the Naval War College," *The American Journal of International Law* 50, no. 3 (1956): 659-63, https://www.jstor.org/stable/2195515?seq=1 (accessed March 26, 2020).
78   Robert Tucker interview.
79   C. Fenwick, Collective Security Under International Law, by Hans Kelsen (U.S. Naval War College, International Law Studies, 1954. Vol. XLIX) (Washington, DC: U.S. Government Printing Office, 1957), in *American Journal of International Law,* 52 (4), p. 811.
80   JL2 interview. "Van Rensselaer Widow Succumbs in Philadelphia," *Newport Daily News,* February 9, 1956. https://www.newspapers.com/clip/25461846/obituary-for-lillian-newlin-van/
81   JL2 interview.
82   JL2 interview.
83   JL2 interview.
84   JL2 interview.
85   JL2 interview.
86   JL2 interview.
87   JL2 interview.
88   Michael Sterner interview.
89   Michael Sterner interview.
90   Michael Sterner interview.
91   JL2 interview.
92   Theodore A. Wilson, *Oral History Interview with Benson E. L. Timmons III,* July 8, 1970. Harry S. Truman Library and Museum, https://www.trumanlibrary.gov/library/oral-histories/timmons.

93 Charles Stuart Kennedy and Albert Ashton Lakeland, Jr., *Interview with Albert Ashton Lakeland, Jr.*, 1992. Manuscript/Mixed Material, https://www.loc.gov/item/mfdipbib000657/.

94 JL2 interview. Dennis Kux and James G. Lowenstein, *Interview with James G. Lowenstein*, 1994, Manuscript/Mixed Material, https://www.loc.gov/item/mfdipbib000720/.

95 JL2 interview.

96 Weisbrode, *The Atlanticists*, p. 189.

97 Sebastian Reyn, *Atlantis Lost: The American Experience with De Gaulle, 1958-1969* (Amsterdam: Amsterdam University Press, 2010), pp. 46-64.

98 Reyn, *Atlantis Lost*, p. 61.

99 JL2 interview.

100 Ceylon was renamed the Democratic Socialist Republic of Sri Lanka in 1972.

101 *Greensboro Daily News*, December 28, 1958.

102 https://www.usaid.gov/sri-lanka/history

103 JLSupp2 interview.

104 JL2 interview.

105 JL2 interview.

106 Charles Stuart Kennedy and Richard E. Johnson, *Interview with Richard E. Johnson*, 1991, Manuscript/Mixed Material, https://www.loc.gov/item/mfdipbib000567/

107 JL2 interview. Kennedy and Dunlop, *Interview with Thomas P. H. Dunlop*. Thomas Niles interview.

108 Charles Stuart Kennedy and Thomas M. T. Niles, *Interview with Thomas M. T. Niles*, 1998, Manuscript/Mixed Material, https://www.adst.org/OH%20TOCs/Niles,%20Thomas%20M.T.toc.pdf. Kennedy and Dunlop, *Interview with Thomas P. H. Dunlop*.

109 JL2 interview.

110 Lees, *Keeping Tito Afloat*, Introduction.

111 Thomas Niles interview. Kennedy and Dunlop, *Interview with Thomas P. H. Dunlop*. Leonard J. Saccio and Lawrence S. Eagleburger, *Interview with Lawrence S. Eagleburger*, 1998, Manuscript/Mixed Material, https://www.adst.org/OH%20TOCs/Eagleburger,%20Lawrence%20S.toc.pdf

112 Kennedy and Dunlop, *Interview with Thomas P. H. Dunlop*.

113 Kennedy and Dunlop, *Interview with Thomas P. H. Dunlop*.

114 James G. Lowenstein, "Yugoslavia: Parliamentary Model?" in *Problems of Communism,* Vol. XIV (January-February 1965), pp. 132-135.

115 JL2 interview.

116 Kennedy and Johnson, *Interview with Richard E. Johnson.*

117 Kennedy and Dunlop, *Interview with Thomas P. H. Dunlop.*

118 Thomas Niles interview.

119 Kennedy and Dunlop, *Interview with Thomas P. H. Dunlop.*

120 Thomas Niles interview. Kennedy and Dunlop, *Interview with Thomas P. H. Dunlop.*

121 JL Vignette.

122 Kennedy and Niles, *Interview with Thomas M. T. Niles.*

123 Charles Stuart Kennedy and Robert Gerald Livingston, *Interview with Robert Gerald Livingston,* 1998. Manuscript/Mixed Material, https://www.loc.gov/item/mfdipbib000703/

124 Ibid.

125 Randall Bennett Woods, *Fulbright: A Biography* (Cambridge University Press, 1995), p. 370. JL2.

126 Kux and Lowenstein, *Interview with James G. Lowenstein.*

Chapter 3

127 JL3 interview.

128 JLSupp2 interview.

129 Marcy oral history

130 Marcy oral history.

131 Memo, Carl Marcy to All Members, Senate Foreign Relations Committee, n.d. Ellen C. Collier, ed., *Bipartisanship And The Making Of Foreign Policy: A Historical Survey* (Routledge, 2018 (1991), Chapter 6.

132 Transcript of Committee meeting, February 9, 1972.

133 JL3 Interview.. Memo, Carl Marcy to All Members, Senate Committee on Foreign Relations, n.d.

134 Memo, Carl Marcy to All Members, Senate Foreign Relations Committee, n.d.

135 Transcript of Committee meeting, February 9, 1972.

136 Pat Holt interview. JL3 Interview. Randall Bennett Woods, *Fulbright: A Biography* (Cambridge University Press, 1995), p. 373. Tillman oral history. JLSupp2.

137 *New York Times,* May 27, 1964.

138 JL3 interview.

139 Kux and Lowenstein, *Interview with James G. Lowenstein*.

140 Memo, Jim Lowenstein to Senator Fulbright, "Hearings on European Problems," March 31, 1966.

141 Memo, Senator Fulbright to Senator Church, March 31, 1966.

142 JL KUX

143 JL4 interview.

144 William J. Fulbright, "Hearings: US policy in Europe," June 1966.

145 JL3 interview.

146 "Frank Church, "U. S. Policy and the New Europe," *Foreign Affairs*, Vol. 45, No. 1 (October 1966), pp. 49-57.

147 Kux and Lowenstein, *Interview with James G. Lowenstein*. James G. Lowenstein, Speech to Conference on the Atlantic Community, Georgetown University, March 17, 1969.

148 Memo, Jim Lowenstein to Senator Pell, September 23, 1968.

149 JL3 interview.

150 Kux and Lowenstein, *Interview with James G. Lowenstein*. JL4 interview.

151 Herring, p. 143.

152 Herring, p. 143.

153 Marcy oral history. Dallek, pp. 219ff. Herring, pp. 150-1.

154 Felten, "The Path to Dissent," p. 1010-1011.

155 Woods, p. 94.

156 Woods, pp. 370-1. Quoted in Felten, "The Path to Dissent," p. 1009.

157 Felten, "The Path to Dissent," p. 1011. Pat Holt oral history. Kux and Lowenstein, *Interview with James G. Lowenstein*.

158 Woods, p. 371. Felten, "The Path to Dissent," p. 1015.

159 Marcy oral history.

160 JL3 interview. Holt oral history.

161 Marcy oral history.

162 Holt oral history. Marcy oral history. Dallek, p. 254.

163 Woods, p. 371.

164 JL3 Interview.

165 Kux and Lowenstein, *Interview with James G. Lowenstein*.

166 Memo, Jim Lowenstein to Senator Fulbright, July 11, 1967.

167 Memo, Jim Lowenstein to Senator Fulbright, July 11, 1967. Kux and Lowenstein, *Interview with James G. Lowenstein*.

168 Kux and Lowenstein, *Interview with James G. Lowenstein*.

169 Dallek, p. 308.

170 McMahon, p. 204.

171 Richard Dudman, "Rosy Vietnam Reports Under Study," *St. Louis Post-Dispatch*, February 1, 1970.

172 Herring, pp. 277ff, p. 289. Woods, p. 536.

173 Memo, Jim Lowenstein to Senator Fulbright, November 6, 1967. JL vignette. Woods, pp. 603-7.

174 Memo, Jim Lowenstein to Norvill Jones, March 23, 1973. Daniel Ellsberg, *Secrets: A Memoir of Vietnam and the Pentagon Papers*, pp. 326-7. Tom Wells, *Wild Man: The Life and Times of Daniel Ellsberg*, p. 404. Marcy oral history. Woods, p. 604.

175 Woods, p. 518.

176 Woods, p. 507. "Change of Tune," *Evening Star*, February 4, 1970.

177 Kux and Lowenstein, *Interview with James G. Lowenstein*. Moose oral history. Woods, p. 550. John W. Finney, "War-Policy Basis Is Called Dubious," *New York Times*, February 2, 1970.

178 Walter Pincus and Thomas W. Lippman, "Intelligence Agency Should Like the Cut of Lake's Coat," *Washington Post*, December 6, 1996.

179 Moose oral history. JL4 interview.

180 Marcy oral history.

181 Moose oral history.

182 JL3 interview.

183 Moose oral history.

184 "Vietnam: 1969", a staff report prepared for the use of the Committee on Foreign Relations, United States Senate (February 2, 1970), p. 3. Moose oral history.

185 "Vietnam: 1969", pp. 1-2.

186 "Change of Tune," *Evening Star*, February 4, 1970.

187 "Vietnam: 1969", p. 8. Woods, pp. 561, 552. "Vietnam: 1969", p. 18.

188 *Wall Street Journal*, February 2, 1970. Marvin Kalb interview. JL3 Interview.

189 Woods, p. 552. Kux and Lowenstein, *Interview with James G. Lowenstein*. Marvin Kalb interview.

190 Letter, George Kennan to James Lowenstein, February 27, 1970.

191 Marcy oral history

192 Memoranda of Conversation, Prince Sihanouk and Senator Mansfield, Royal Palace, Phnom Penh, August 22, 1969. Kux and Lowenstein, *Interview with James G. Lowenstein*.

193 Kux and Lowenstein, *Interview with James G. Lowenstein*. Herring, pp. 296ff.

194 Kux and Lowenstein, *Interview with James G. Lowenstein*. Memo, Jim Lowenstein and Dick Moose to Carl Marcy, April 22, 1970. Moose oral history.

195 Memo, Jim Lowenstein and Dick Moose to Senator Fulbright, May 7, 1970 (filed May 3).

196 "Cambodia: December 1970," A Staff Report. December 16, 1970.

197 Herring, pp. 301-2.

198 Memo, Jim Lowenstein and Dick Moose to Senator Fulbright, October 14, 1970, p. 1. Moose oral history.

199 Louis Fisher, "Presidential Spending Discretion and Congressional Controls," *Law and Contemporary Problems*, vol. 37, no. 1, 1972, p. 144.

200 Memo, Jim Lowenstein and Dick Moose to Senator Fulbright, October 14, 1970, p. 7.

201 Memo, Jim Lowenstein and Dick Moose to Senator Fulbright, October 14, 1970.

202 Memo, Jim Lowenstein and Dick Moose to Carl Marcy, November 16, 1970.

203 Carl M. Marcy, letter to the editor, *Washington Daily News,* February 9, 1971.

204 John W. Finney, "Senate Unit Backs Aid for Cambodia But Bars Troops," *New York Times*, December 15, 1970.

205 Kux and Lowenstein, *Interview with James G. Lowenstein*. Frederick Poole, "Congress v. Kissinger: The New Equalizers," *The Washington Monthly,* May 1975, pp. 23ff. Julian Manyon, "Senate Probers Turn On at Phnom Penh Party," *New York Daily News*, December 16, 1970. JLSupp3 interview. "Finding the Facts with L&M," *Newsweek*, June 25, 1973.

206 Woods, pp. 587-8.

207 *Newsweek*, January 4, 1971. Terence Smith, "Senators Receive Hanoi P.O.W. List," *New York Times,* December 23, 1970.

208 *Newsweek*, January 4, 1971. Terence Smith, "Senators Receive Hanoi P.O.W. List," *New York Times*, December 23, 1970.

209 *Newsweek*, January 4, 1971. Terence Smith, "Senators Receive Hanoi P.O.W. List," *New York Times*, December 23, 1970. Memo, Jim Lowenstein to Senator Aiken, December 23, 1970.

210 Woods, p. 590. Rowland Evans and Robert Novak, "Sen. Fulbright vs. the Junta," *The Washington Post*, January 31, 1971.

211 Letter, Senator J. W. Fulbright to William P. Rogers, [February 25, 1971].

212 Kux and Lowenstein, *Interview with James G. Lowenstein*.

213 Greece report, pp. 14-5.

214 "Korea and the Philippines: November 1972." John W. Finney, "Anti-Marcos Plot Detailed in U.S." *International Herald Tribune*, February 19, 1973. Stanley Karnow, *In Our Image: America's Empire in the Philippines* (New York: Random House, 1989), pp. 380-1.

215 Habib oral history. JL3

216 "Korea and the Philippines: November 1972," a staff report prepared for the use of the Committee on Foreign Relations United States Senate, February 18, 1973, p. 47.

217 Woods, p. 528. Herring, pp. 305ff.

218 Woods, p. 552. "Laos: April 1971," A Staff Report Prepared For The Use Of The Subcommittee on U.S. Security Agreements And Commitments Abroad Of The Committee On Foreign Relations United States Senate (Washington: U.S. Government Printing Office), August 3, 1971. Laurence Stern, "Deeper CIA Role in Laos Revealed," *The Washington Post*, August 3, 1971.

219 "Thailand, Laos, and Cambodia: January 1972," A Staff Report Prepared For The Use Of The Subcommittee on U.S. Security Agreements And Commitments Abroad Of The Committee On Foreign Relations United States Senate (Washington: U.S. Government Printing Office), May 8, 1972. *Washington Post*, May 13, 1972.

220 Letter, Stuart Symington to John C. Stennis, Chairman, Armed Services Committee, April 5, 1972.

221 Herring, pp. 307ff.

222 Memo, Senator Fulbright to Senator Aiken, May 11, 1972.

223 "Vietnam: May 1972," a staff report prepared for the use of the Committee on Foreign Relations United States Senate, June 29, 1972. John W. Finney, "Defense Department Subsidy to Saigon is Charged," *New York Times*, June 29, 1972. Stanley Karnow, "Senate Study Finds

Saigon Regime Might Not Survive a Cease-Fire," *The Washington Post*, June 29, 1972.

224 "Vietnam: May 1972," a staff report prepared for the use of the Committee on Foreign Relations United States Senate, June 29, 1972. John W. Finney, "Defense Department Subsidy to Saigon is Charged," *New York Times*, June 29, 1972. Stanley Karnow, "Senate Study Finds Saigon Regime Might Not Survive a Cease-Fire," *The Washington Post*, June 29, 1972.

225 William Shawcross, "No peace, no honour," *Far Eastern Economic Review*, July 9, 1973.

226 Memo, Jim Lowenstein and Dick Moose to Carl Marcy, May 18, 1973.

227 "Thailand, Laos, Cambodia, and Vietnam: April 1973," a staff report prepared for the use of the Committee on Foreign Relations United States Senate, June 11, 1973, p. 45. Bruce Palling, "Laos: Ending a CIA War," *Far Eastern Economic Review*, July 9, 1973.

228 "U.S. Air Operations In Cambodia: April 1973," a staff report prepared for the use of the Committee on Foreign Relations United States Senate, April 27, 1973, p. 1. Stuart Symington, quoted in Randall Bennett Woods, *J. William Fulbright, Vietnam, and the Search for a Cold War Foreign Policy* (Cambridge University Press, 1998), p. 271. Michael Getler, "Air Strikes At 240 a Day In Cambodia," *The Washington Post*, April 28, 1973. Rudy Abramson, "Cambodia Bombing Seen U.S. Directed," *Los Angeles Times*, April 28, 1973.

229 Frederick Poole, "Congress v. Kissinger: The New Equalizers," *The Washington Monthly*, May 1975, pp. 23ff. Charles W. Bailey, "Senate Aides Expose Nixon Bombing Policy," *Minneapolis Tribune*, May 13, 1973. Richard L. Madden, "Sweeping Cutoff of Funds for War is Voted in Senate," *New York Times*, June 15, 1973. Woods, pp. 633, 636.

230 Murrey Marder, "Senate Report Analyzes U.S. Nuclear Force in Europe," The Washington Post, December 2, 1973.

231 JL3 interview. Moose oral history.

232 JL3 interview. Marvin Kalb interview. "Finding the Facts with L&M," *Newsweek*, June 25, 1973, p. 38.

233 *The Evening Star*, December 24, 1970. Stanley Karnow, "The Kissinger-Fulbright Courtship," *The New Republic* (December 29, 1973).

234 Kux and Lowenstein, *Interview with James G. Lowenstein*.

235 Moose oral history. JL3 interview. Kux and Lowenstein, *Interview with James G. Lowenstein*.

236 JL3 interview. Kux and Lowenstein, *Interview with James G. Lowenstein*. Memo, Jim Lowenstein and Dick Moose to Senator Fulbright, October 14, 1970, p. 6.

237 Moose oral history

238 Kux and Lowenstein, *Interview with James G. Lowenstein*.

239 JL3 interview.

240 Kux and Lowenstein, *Interview with James G. Lowenstein*. Herring, p. 307.

241 Kux and Lowenstein, *Interview with James G. Lowenstein*.

242 JL3 interview.

243 Kux and Lowenstein, *Interview with James G. Lowenstein*.

244 "Thailand, Laos, and Cambodia: January 1972," A Staff Report Prepared For The Use Of The Subcommittee on U.S. Security Agreements And Commitments Abroad Of The Committee On Foreign Relations United States Senate (Washington: U.S. Government Printing Office), May 8, 1972. Press release, Senator Stuart Symington, May 8, 1972. John W. Finney, "U.S. Pledge for Thai Units in Laos Put at $100-Million," *New York Times*, May 8, 1972. Laurence Stern, "Thai Force in Laos Financed by U. S., Secret Report Says," *Washington Post*, May 8, 1972. "Fighting in Laos, Cambodia Growing, Hill Report Warns," *Washington Post*, March 2, 1972. "Report Bares Role of U.S. in Laos," *The Evening Star*, May 8, 1972.

245 Moose oral history. Woods, pp. 628-9.

246 William Shawcross, *Sideshow: Kissinger, Nixon, and the Destruction of Cambodia* (Simon & Schuster, 1979), p. 276.

247 Woods, pp. 630-1. JL3 interview.

248 Kux and Lowenstein, *Interview with James G. Lowenstein*.

249 Marvin Kalb interview.

250 Winston Lord interview. Moose oral history.

251 Winston Lord interview. Moose oral history.

252 Included as part of Memo, Carl Marcy to All Members of the Committee on Foreign Relations, April 4, 1972.

253 Holt oral history.

254 Memorandum, Lowenstein and Moose to Fulbright, December 20, 1972.

Chapter 4
255 Transcript of Committee meeting, February 9, 1972.

256 Kux and Lowenstein, *Interview with James G. Lowenstein*.

257 Kux and Lowenstein, *Interview with James G. Lowenstein*. JL4 interview.

258 "Critic Slips Back To State," *Washington Start-News*, April 10, 1974. Kux and Lowenstein, *Interview with James G. Lowenstein*.

259 Letter, Jim Lowenstein to Senator Stuart Symington, March 27, 1974. Letter, Jim Lowenstein to Senator J. W. Fulbright, March 27, 1974.

260 Moose oral history. Kux and Lowenstein, *Interview with James G. Lowenstein*.

261 Kux and Lowenstein, *Interview with James G. Lowenstein*. JL4 interview.

262 Winston Lord interview. Kux and Lowenstein, *Interview with James G. Lowenstein*.

263 JL4 interview. Kux and Lowenstein, *Interview with James G. Lowenstein*. William D. Miller and Arthur A. Hartman, *Interview with Arthur A. Hartman*, 1989. Manuscript/Mixed Material, https://www.loc.gov/item/mfdipbib000487/.

264 Kux and Lowenstein, *Interview with James G. Lowenstein*.

265 JL4 interview.

266 Bremer oral history.

267 Vest oral history.

268 JL4 interview. Kux and Lowenstein, *Interview with James G. Lowenstein*.

269 Kux and Lowenstein, *Interview with James G. Lowenstein*. JL Vignette.

270 JL4 interview. Kux and Lowenstein, *Interview with James G. Lowenstein*.

271 JL4 interview.

272 L. Paul Bremer oral history. Winston Lord oral history. Joseph Sisco oral history.

273 Kux and Lowenstein, *Interview with James G. Lowenstein*.

274 Kux and Lowenstein, *Interview with James G. Lowenstein*. JL4 interview.

275 James G. Lowenstein, "The French-American Foundation: Early Years," https://frenchamerican.org/wp-content/uploads/early-years.pdf. Yves-Andre Istel interview.

276 Lowenstein, "The French-American Foundation." Francois Bujon interview.

277 JL3 interview.

278 Kux and Lowenstein, *Interview with James G. Lowenstein*. Charles Stuart Kennedy and Arthur Adair Hartman, *Interview with Arthur Adair Hartman*, 1999, https://adst.org/wp-content/uploads/2013/12/Hartman-Arthur-Adair.pdf, JL4 interview.

279 Kux and Lowenstein, *Interview with James G. Lowenstein*. Martin Tolchin, Choice of Ambassadors a Constant Point of Dispute Between Professional and Politician," *New York Times*, May 18, 1979.

280 Kux and Lowenstein, *Interview with James G. Lowenstein*.

281 JL4 interview.

282 Paul Helminger interview. Robert G. Kaiser, "Luxembourg May Get Its Wish – A Career Diplomat as an Envoy," *The Washington Post*, April 26, 1977. Lawrence Van Gelder, "Ruth Farkas, 89, Nixon's Ambassador to Luxembourg, Dies," *New York Times*, October 22, 1996.

283 Robert G. Kaiser, "Luxembourg May Get Its Wish – A Career Diplomat as an Envoy," *The Washington Post*, April 26, 1977. Paul Helminger interview. JL vignette.

284 Kux and Lowenstein, *Interview with James G. Lowenstein*. JL4 interview.

285 "Background Notes: Luxembourg," Department of State, February 1978.

286 Higginson oral history. De Muyser oral history.

287 JL4

288 Kux and Lowenstein, *Interview with James G. Lowenstein*.Charles Higginson interview.

289 Kux and Lowenstein, *Interview with James G. Lowenstein*.Charles Higginson interview.

290 Kux and Lowenstein, *Interview with James G. Lowenstein*. JL4 interview. Paul Helminger interview.

291 Kux and Lowenstein, *Interview with James G. Lowenstein*.

292 JL4 interview. Higginson interview.

293 JL4 interview. Kux and Lowenstein, *Interview with James G. Lowenstein*.

294 JL4 interview.

295 Kux and Lowenstein, *Interview with James G. Lowenstein*. Marshall Wais interview.

296 Kux and Lowenstein, *Interview with James G. Lowenstein*. Higginson oral history.

297 Wanda Kennicott interview.

298 Colette Flesch interview. Guy De Muyser interview. Paul Helminger interview.

299 Kux and Lowenstein, *Interview with James G. Lowenstein*. Myriam Norris interview.

300 JL4 interview.

301 Kux and Lowenstein, *Interview with James G. Lowenstein*. JL4 interview. Paul Helminger interview. Colette Flesch interview.

302 Kux and Lowenstein, *Interview with James G. Lowenstein*.

303 Guy De Muyser interview. Colette Flesch interview. Paul Helminger interview.

304 Kux and Lowenstein, *Interview with James G. Lowenstein*.

305 Kux and Lowenstein, *Interview with James G. Lowenstein*.

306 Kux and Lowenstein, *Interview with James G. Lowenstein*.

307 Kux and Lowenstein, *Interview with James G. Lowenstein*.

Epilogue

308 JLSupp3 interview. Michael Sterner interview.

309 JLSupp3 interview.

310 JLSupp3 interview. Michael Sterner interview.

311 JLSupp3 interview. *Independent,* February 4, 1997, https://www.independent.co.uk/news/people/obituary-nikola-koljevic-1276825.html. Raymond Bonner, "Rising Bosnian Serb Leader Offers Accord Rare Praise," *New York Times,* November 26, 1995, https://www.nytimes.com/1995/11/26/world/rising-bosnian-serb-leader-offers-accord-rare-praise.html.

312 John Kavanagh, "Hope Rises as the Wall Falls," *Financial Review,* December 1, 1989, https://www.afr.com/companies/hopes-rise-as-the-wall-falls-19891201-kajh4. JLSupp4 interview.

313 JLSupp3 interview. John D. Chapman interview. "No confidence," *Economist,* August 2, 1997, https://www.economist.com/finance-and-economics/1997/07/31/no-confidence. "New Funds Focus on Ukraine, As Money Managers See Value," *Wall Street Journal,* May 16, 1997, https://www.wsj.com/articles/SB863802636342292500.

314 JLSupp3 interview. François Bujon interview. Yves-André Istel interview. Charles Stuart Kennedy and Arthur Adair Hartman, *Interview with Arthur Adair Hartman,* 1999, https://adst.org/wp-content/uploads/2013/12/Hartman-Arthur-Adair.pdf.

315 "Entre Paris et New York, des amitiés très élitistes," *Les Echos,* October 10, 2012, http://archives.lesechos.fr/archives/2012/Enjeux/00294-033-ENJ.htm. Young Leaders 2012 Program Description.

316 Vivien de Gunzburg interview. Shannon Fairbanks interview. Jean-Luc Allavena interview.

317 Yves-André Istel interview. François Bujon interview.

318 Shannon Fairbanks interview. Jean-Luc Allavena interview.
319 Marvin Kalb interview.
320 Marvin Kalb interview.
321 Laurinda Douglas interview.

Made in the USA
Middletown, DE
07 September 2021